# THE GREEK FEAST

# THE
# GREEK
# FEAST

*Santa Barbara Style*

A Collection of Family Recipes from
Saint Barbara Greek Orthodox Church

OLYMPUS PRESS
SANTA BARBARA • 1999

*In appreciation to*
*Rev. Constantine Zozos*
*and the Parish Council*
*for their support of this project.*

Published by Olympus Press
John McKinney, *Publisher*
Post Office Box 2397, Santa Barbara,
California 93120-2397

Cheri Rae McKinney, *Editor*
Vivian Pahos and Andriana
Kolendrianos, and Mary Papador-
Mendoza, *Technical Consultants*

Design and typography by Jim Cook
Cover illustrations by Merv Corning
from Santa Barbara Greek Festival
posters

# CONTENTS

# INTRODUCTION

SANTA BARBARA is well known as a beautiful, Mediterranean-style community located on the scenic California coast. It's less well known, but still significant, as home to a diverse population—including a thriving Greek community. The heart of this Greek community—indeed its very soul—resides within the congregation of Saint Barbara Greek Orthodox Church.

For more than a quarter-century, members of the congregation have shared the Greek culture with all of Santa Barbara at the annual Santa Barbara Greek Festival. Year after year, festival-goers ask for the recipes for savory meats, tasty salads, and fantastic desserts. Gathered here are many of the festival favorites, along with scores of traditional family recipes for Greek feasts you can prepare at home. There are dishes and desserts from throughout the Mediterranean region—from Cephalonia to Constantinople, from Salonika to Sparta—and all points in between.

Some recipes have been adapted to the Santa Barbara lifestyle—a little avocado here, some sun-dried tomatoes there. But by and large, the recipes collected here are the delectable, traditional home-cooked Greek flavors familiar to those lucky enough to grow up in a Greek family—or live close to one!

We invite you to try these dishes, and hope

you enjoy them as much as we have enjoyed discovering, collecting and presenting them to you.

A traditional Greek compliment to the cook translates to "Bless your hands." May you and your guests be always grateful, ever-blessed.

Thanks go for the efforts of many individuals who assisted with and contributed to this book. They include:

The Committee: Kathy Gallo, Georgia Gastouniotis, Valerie Katsikis, Andriana Kolendrianos, Vivian Pahos, Mary Papador-Mendoza, Kathy Poulos, Georgia Papador, and Helen Stathis.

Contributors include Voula Aldrich, Anne Athanassakis, Angie Andropoulos, Anna Apostolos, Galatea Constantinides, Jean Futris, Helen Goumas, Cynthia Jensen, Irene Lendaris, Gloria Menedes, Mary Mikos, Mike Pahos, Vasiliki Pappas, Stella Pollalis, Clara Prodromos, Alexandra Scarvelis, George Scarvelis, Alexandra Sfaelos-Iorio, Mary Stamos, Helen Stathopoulos, Art Trigonis, Katherine Trigonis, Delight Vames, Sam Velliotes, and Mariann Zacharellis.

—CHERI RAE MCKINNEY

# APPETIZERS

A. Ταρσούλη.

# Cheese Triangles (Tiropitakia)

*A traditional cheese pastry characterized by golden, flaky filo dough which makes for an elegant appetizer.*

Cream cheeses well. Add eggs. Cut filo sheets into long strips, 3 inches wide. Butter each strip. Fold corner over filling to make a triangle. Continue folding in triangular shape until entire strip is folded. Place on buttered baking sheet and brush with butter. Bake at 350 degrees for 15 to 20 minutes. Always serve warm. Yield: 50 pieces.

**Note:** This may be prepared instead, in a 9×13-inch pan using half a pound of filo dough, layering half in bottom of buttered pan, brushing each sheet with butter, add the filling and top with remaining filo dough, brushing each sheet with butter. Score top before baking at 350 degrees for 30 to 35 minutes. Cool slightly, cut into squares and serve warm.

1/2 pound feta cheese, crumbled
1 cup small curd cottage cheese
3 ounces cream cheese
3 eggs, beaten
1/2 pound unsalted butter, melted
1 pound filo dough

## STOCKING A GREEK KITCHEN

The foremost ingredient is **Greek oregano**—the most flavorful and fragrant oregano available. Other essential ingredients are **extra virgin olive oil**, **fresh garlic**, fresh or dried **dill weed**, **rosemary**, **bay leaves**, **fresh lemon juice**, **mastiha crystals** (from the island of Hios), which can be found in Greek-Italian import food stores. Mastiha makes the most flavorful, aromatic Easter and New Year's breads. **Filo** in your freezer, **sweet butter**, **brandy**, **honey**, **cinnamon** (ground and sticks), **cumin**, **sesame seeds**, **cloves**, and **allspice** for baking. **Greek coffee** and a **brika** (traditional long-handled, cylindrical copper or brass pot; today stainless is preferable); dried legumes, such as **lentils**, **navy beans**, **garbanzos**, or **large limas**.

**Supplies:** large baking or **roasting pans** (11×17-inch or, preferably, 12×18-inch, which can be found in a good kitchen supply or restaurant supply shop) for pastitsio, moussaka, baklava; a **food processor** for the creamiest sauces and dips; a **candy thermometer** for the perfect, no-guess-work baklava syrup.

# Spinach Triangles with Feta (Spanakopitakia)

*No cocktail party would be complete without this natural companion to the cheese triangle. Today's busy cook might want to substitute frozen spinach—use two 10-ounce packages thawed and squeezed dry.*

2 bunches spinach
2 bunches green onions
1/2 cup olive oil
1 pound feta cheese crumbled
4 eggs, well beaten
1/2 cup chopped parsley
1/4 teaspoon dill weed
1 pound filo dough
1 pound unsalted butter, melted

Clean and chop spinach, salt well and place in colander to drain thoroughly. Squeeze out excess moisture from spinach and place in large bowl. Chop green onions and sauté in oil until wilted and add to spinach. Add cheese and seasonings being careful not to oversalt since feta is salty. Add eggs and blend well. Cut filo into long strips, 3 inches wide, and brush with melted butter. Place 1 teaspoon filling on one end of pastry strip and fold over to make a triangle. Continue folding in triangular shape until entire strip is used. Place on baking sheet, brush with butter. Bake at 350 degrees for 15 to 20 minutes, until lightly browned. Serve warm.

**Note:** These spinach triangles can be frozen until ready to bake. Place on baking sheet and chill until easily handled. Then pack closely in pan or box, in layers divided with wax paper. Seal securely and freeze. It is not necessary to defrost before baking; just bake a little longer if frozen.

# Artichoke Appetizers (Anginares Yia Orektika)

*This recipe results in a frittata-like appetizer with a quiche-type texture and a delicate artichoke and Fontinella flavor.*

This works very easily with a food processor. Drain artichoke hearts, reserving liquid; and chop. Combine grated (or shredded) cheese, onion, garlic, parsley, cracker crumbs in large mixing bowl. Beat eggs, add to above mixture with artichoke hearts, reserved marinade, and seasonings. Taste for salt and pepper if you wish. Turn into oiled 9×13-inch pan and bake at 325 degrees.

3 jars (6 ounces each) marinated artichoke hearts
1 1/2 cups chopped green onion
1 1/2 cups chopped parsley
2 cloves garlic, minced
8 eggs, beaten
12 soda crackers, crumbled
2 7-ounce sticks Fontinella cheese
dash hot pepper sauce
dash Worcestershire sauce
salt and pepper (if desired)

## HOW TO HANDLE FILO

The paper thin pastry used in Greek pastries, known as filo or phyllo, is available in one-pound packages, frozen or unfrozen, in many supermarkets and Greek and Italian specialty stores. When working with filo to keep filo from drying out, keep it covered with plastic wrap or waxed paper and a damp towel. Also keep doors and windows closed to prevent drafts from drying out your filo as you work. Do not unwrap filo until ready to use. Filo can be kept frozen for several months.
It is very important when using frozen filo to thaw it slowly so condensation does not form inside the wrapped package of pastry, causing the filo sheets to stick together. Eight hours in the refrigerator from the freezer then four hours at room temperature is a reliable rule to follow. Unfrozen filo requires only warming to room temperature.

# Feta Crisps

*Feta cheese lovers will love this simple, tasty recipe! Have the dough rolls on hand in your freezer—just slice and bake for your unexpected guests.*

2 cups flour
1/2 teaspoon dried dill weed
2 sticks unsalted butter
1/2 pound feta cheese crumbled
1 egg

Combine the flour with dill weed and set aside. In a food processor, mix the butter and cheese until mealy. Add the flour mixture and pulse 2 to 3 times, add egg and process until blended and holds its shape. Be careful not to overprocess mixture.

Shape into two rolls wrapped in wax paper and store in freezer overnight, or until needed.

Heat oven to 350 degrees. Cut dough roll into ¼-inch slices and place on ungreased cookie sheet. Bake for about 20 to 25 minutes, until lightly browned. Serve warm.

Makes about 5 dozen crisps.

# Saganaki

*This flaming appetizer will make a dramatic entrance at your next gathering.*

Cut well-chilled kasseri cheese into ¾-inch cubes. Coat cheese cubes with egg mixture and dredge through bread crumbs to coat entire cube. Place breaded cheese cubes on to waxed paper and separate second layer with another piece of waxed paper. Cover and refrigerate at least one hour.

Heat large nonstick skillet. Coat bottom of skillet with olive oil. When oil is hot, drop in chilled cheese cubes and quickly sauté tossing pan to brown all sides. Once cubes are browned pour in cognac and ignite. Douse the flames by squeezing fresh lemon juice over flaming cheese serve at once right from the pan with long toothpicks.

**Note:** If cheese is cooked too long it will melt, lose its cubed shape, and become impossible to serve.

1 pound kasseri cheese
seasoned Italian bread crumbs
2 eggs slightly beaten
best quality olive oil
1/4 cup cognac or brandy
Lemon wedges

# Caviar Potato Dip (Taramosalata)

*Tarama is typically sold in specialty import shops or delis in jars of ten to sixteen ounces. Float a layer of oil on top and refrigerate remainder until next use.*

6 to 8 ounces tarama (fish roe)
6 boiled potatoes, medium
1 onion
1 cup olive oil
juice of three medium lemons

Squeeze bread well. Place tarama in blender jar and blend at low speed until smooth and creamy. Add onions and bread and blend at high speed until light and creamy. Add olive oil and lemon juice and blend at low speed until well mixed. Place in salad bowl and garnish with chopped parsley and black olives.

May be used as a dip or spread. Also good for stuffing cherry tomatoes, cucumbers or avocados.

## HOW TO CURE OLIVES

Olive Street in downtown Santa Barbara is lined with (what else?) olive trees. The silvery gray leaves on the graceful trees provide lovely shade, but the olives on the sidewalk make it slippery at times. The smartest residents collect the olives before they drop—and cure them as follows:

Collect olives when ripe. Slash each olive with a knife, then soak in cold water for ten days to two weeks, changing the water daily to remove the bitterness of raw olives. After ten days, taste to see that bitterness is gone. If not, continue soaking up to two weeks. Cover with a brine solution of one cup salt to one quart water for twenty-four hours, then wash off the brine and drain. Store in jars with mixture of olive oil and red wine vinegar and flavored with any or all of the following: garlic slivers, oregano leaves, celery sticks, coriander seeds. Store in refrigerator.

# Taramosalata

*The elegance of caviar on a modest budget, this bright orange carp roe allows you to serve this any time. With the added ease of the food processor, it is also easy to prepare. For a California twist to this dip, mash a large avocado and blend with a cup of taramosalata—call it "taramole."*

Squeeze bread well. Place tarama in blender jar and blend at low speed until smooth and creamy. Add onions and bread and blend at high speed until light and creamy. Add olive oil and lemon juice and blend at low speed until well mixed. Place in salad bowl and garnish with chopped parsley and black olives.

May be used as a dip or spread. Also good for stuffing cherry tomatoes, cucumbers or avocados.

**Note:** To increase proportions, use one slice of bread per ounce of tarama.

1 5-ounce jar tarama (fish roe)
2 cups bread, soaked (no crusts)
1 small onion, chopped
1 cup olive oil
juice of two lemons

## PROCESSOR METHOD:

In processor bowl, whirl 5 slices white bread to make crumbs, add water and onion and process until chopped. Add tarama and process until smooth, then add lemon juice. With machine running, slowly add olive oil in a fine stream. Process until smooth and light pink. If you prefer a milder tasting taramosalata, add more bread which has been soaked in water and squeezed dry. You can even add more lemon juice or olive oil for personal taste

**Processor Method:**
5 ounces tarama
5 slices white bread, crusts removed
water as needed
1 small onion, quartered
1/4 cup lemon juice
1 cup olive oil

# Athenian Eggplant Salad (Melitzanosalata)

*A wonderful side dish, salsa-like in texture. Eggplant can be baked in the microwave; wrap securely and bake until soft.*

1 small eggplant (about 3/4 pound)
1 to 2 cloves garlic, coarsely chopped
1/4 medium onion, coarsely chopped
2 tablespoons chopped fresh Italian parsley
1/4 teaspoon chopped fresh mint leaves
1/2 teaspoon dried Greek oregano
1 1/2 teaspoons wine vinegar
juice of one lemon
1/4 cup olive oil
1/8 teaspoon salt

Heat oven to 450 degrees. Prick the eggplant once with the point of a knife and place it on a baking sheet in the oven. Roast until soft all the way through to the center, about 50 minutes. Set aside to cool for 10 minutes or so. When cool enough to handle, slit open and scrape out the pulp. Coarsely chop and transfer to a bowl.

Add remaining ingredients to bowl and stir to blend. Serve with pita bread.

# Feta & Kalamata Olive Mezedes

*This is a fast, elegant and flavorful hors d'oeuvre that will please any crowd.*

crisp cucumbers or water crackers
goat cheese
Kalamata olives finely chopped
Roma tomato chopped
green onion
dill

Slice cucumbers into discs and spread with goat cheese, then with Kalamata olives. Decorate each appetizer with a sprig of dill and small pieces of tomato and green onion.

# Stuffed Grapevine Leaves (Dolmathakia)

*The custom of using grapevine leaves to wrap bits of food dates back to the time of Alexander the Great. Today's hostess would not think of having a cocktail party or buffet without a platter of stuffed grapevine leaves garnished with fresh lemons. It is well worth the effort since there is no equal to homemade dolmathakia.*

Bring about 3 cups water to a boil; add rice and remove from heat. Sauté onions in oil until limp. Drain rice, add to onions, add dill, parsley, mint, salt and pepper; mix well and sauté additional 5 minutes. Remove from heat, add lemon juice and allow to cool.

1 1/2 cups raw rice (not converted)
3 cups chopped onions
1 cup olive oil
3/4 cup fresh dill, chopped or 2 tablespoons. dry dill weed
3/4 cup fresh parsley, chopped
1/4 cup fresh mint, chopped
2 tsp. salt
1 scant teaspoon pepper
1/2 cup lemon juice
1 2-pound jar grapevine leaves

Blanch grapevine leaves in hot water, drain and spread gently on flat surface keeping the dull side of leaf facing up. Cut off stem and place a teaspoon of filling at base of leaf. Fold up and over the filling from stem end, then fold the right side of the leaf over the filling, then the left side over that, then roll tightly away from you towards the tip of the leaf, into a sausage shape. Place closely in a 6-quart pot lined with grapevine leaves. Repeat until all filling is used. You should have about three layers. Cover with additional leaves and place an inverted plate over dolmathes to keep them from moving during cooking. Add 2 cups boiling water, cover pot, bring to boil then reduce heat and simmer for about 1 hour; until most liquid is absorbed. Allow to cool in pot. Remove plate and gently transfer dolmathes to serving platter. Sprinkle with additional lemon juice and garnish with lemon slices and parsley sprigs. Serve at room temperature or slightly chilled.

These keep well in refrigerator 4 to 5 days. Yield about 60 dolmathes.

For variety, you can add toasted pine nuts, chopped sun-dried tomatoes or white raisins with the cooked rice.

# Tomato & Rice Stuffed Grape Leaves (Dolmathakia)

*A modern adaptation with sun-dried tomatoes.*

2 cups uncooked converted rice
  (brown rice may be used)
1 cup oil (1/2 olive and 1/2 canola)
1 small red onion chopped
1 bunch green onion
1/2 cup Italian parsley chopped
1/4 cup fresh mint or 2
  tablespoons dry mint, chopped
1/3 cup fresh dill, chopped
16-ounce can whole peeled
  tomatoes with juice
1/2 cup sun-dried tomatoes,
  soaked and chopped
8-ounce can tomato sauce
juice of one lemon for mixture
two lemons for later
salt and pepper to taste or season
  with Cavender's Greek
  seasoning
1/2 cup of water
2 to 3 8-ounce jars grape leaves

**Filling:** (Can be made the night before)

Cook the onions together dry in a nonstick pan until clear. Add oils, rice, spices ½ cup water to pan and simmer for 20 to 25 minutes stirring occasionally. If using brown rice, simmer for 40 to 45 minutes.

Remove grape leaves from jar and rinse well in hot water to remove brine. Place leaf, smooth side down, on a plate or board: (if stem is long snip off with scissors). Place 1 teaspoon meat mixture in center of leaf. Starting at stem end, roll and enclose filling carefully. Arrange the filled leaves (dolmathes) in compact layers. Change the direction of the rolls with each layer. Place a heavy dish over rolls to prevent their breaking during cooking. Add warm water and juice from two lemons to cover rolls. cover pan with aluminum foil and cook at 350 degrees for 45 to 50 minutes. When cool, drain off liquid and arrange in serving dish. Decorate with fresh dill and lemon slices. Served chilled or at room temperature.

# Feta Cheese Dip

*This crowd-pleasing tasty dip makes a generous three cups—and it goes fast!*

In food processor, chop garlic fine. Add feta cheese and mix until crumbly. Blend in the cream cheese, then add the yogurt and process until smooth. If too thick, add more yogurt until desired consistency. Add the onion, dill, oregano and pepper and blend. Taste for salt, if needed. Place in bowl and chill until ready to serve with crackers or pita wedges.

For a thicker spread, use 3 to 4 tablespoons yogurt.

**Note:** To lessen the calories of this spread, you can substitute nonfat cottage cheese or tofu for half the cream cheese and process until smooth.

2 8-ounce pkgs. cream cheese at room temperature
8 ounce feta cheese
1/2 cup nonfat yogurt
1 or 2 cloves garlic
3 green onions chopped, or 1/2 teaspoon dried minced onion
2 teaspoons dried dill weed
1 teaspoon dried oregano leaves
3 to 4 twists of freshly ground black pepper

# Hummus

*A popular dip, high in protein, a favorite with vegetarians.*

Soak beans overnight, drain and cover with fresh water in saucepot. Cook for 1 hour, or until soft. Prepare tahini sauce.

Combine remaining ingredients and whirl in blender with enough water until the consistency of molasses. Set aside.

Drain cooked beans and either press through a seive or grind in food processor until smooth. With machine running, slowly add tahini sauce, until thick. Serve chilled, drizzled with olive oil and warmed pita bread.

1 cup dried garbanzo beans
1/2 cup tahini (found in ethnic market or health food store)
1/2 cup fresh lemon juice
1/4 cup (approx) water
2 to 4 cloves garlic, crushed
1 tablespoon white vinegar
dash cumin, to taste
dash red pepper, to taste

# Feta Salsa Dip

*A combination of traditional Greek flavors with a California flair for entertaining. Try serving it with wedges of warm pita bread.*

1 pound feta cheese, crumbled
1 cup extra virgin olive oil
6 green onions, chopped
1/2 cup chopped fresh parsley
3 to 4 large tomatoes, peeled, seeded and chopped
1 cup pitted, chopped Greek olives
1/4 cup fresh lemon juice
1 tablespoon dried oregano
2 teaspoons dried dill or 3 tablespoons chopped fresh dill
ground pepper to taste

With metal blade in food processor, process all ingredients with on-off motions until coarsely blended. Taste to adjust seasonings. Chill for at least 30 minutes before serving.

Can be prepared up to two weeks in advance and refrigerated.

# Greek Pizza

*The perfect combination of Mediterranean flavor and presentation.*

pita bread
olive oil
oregano
tomato slices
feta
Kalamata olives

For a quick "Greek" snack treat, brush a pita bread with olive oil, sprinkle with oregano, and top with slices of tomato, crumbled feta cheese and chopped Kalamata olives. Or garnish with your favorite toppings. Place in toaster oven until hot.

# SAUCES

# Béchamel Sauce I

*According to Athenaeus, author of The Philosophy of Dining, this basic white sauce was first whipped up by a Greek chef named Orion more than 2,000 years ago and is one of the world's classic recipes. Ancient Greeks used it frequently over fish, vegetables and various meats, but modern Greek cooks customarily use it as a topping on casseroles, especially moussaka and pastitsio. Here are two variations on the classic, creamy topping that complements many Greek dishes.*

**I:**
4 tablespoons butter
1/4 teaspoon white pepper
6 tablespoons flour
dash of nutmeg (optional, but delicious)
1 teaspoon salt
2 cups milk

Melt butter over a low heat in a medium saucepan. Add flour, salt, pepper and nutmeg. Stir until well blended. This looks thick and perhaps a little crumbly because there are more dry than liquid ingredients.

Remove from heat. Gradually stir in milk, using a wire whisk, and return to the low heat. Cook, stirring constantly, until thick and smooth. Makes 2 cups.

**Note:** Enrich this sauce by adding ½ to 1 cup grated kefalotiri or kasseri cheese to the sauce after it becomes thick and smooth.

# Béchamel Sauce II

*This is a thinner version of the classic sauce.*

**II:**
2 tablespoons butter
3 tablespoons flour
2 cups heated milk (or 2 cups white stock)
salt and pepper

In heavy saucepan, melt butter over low heat and blend in flour. Cook slowly stirring constantly for about 2 minutes. This will keep your sauce from having a pasty taste. Gradually blend in warmed liquid, stirring with wire whisk until smooth. Cook and stir over medium heat until sauce thickens and comes to a boil, stirring constantly. Salt and pepper to taste.

**Note:** This sauce can be adjusted to suit a variety of entrees. For fish, substitute fish stock for half the milk, for fowl, substitute chicken stock.

# Yogurt (Yiaourti)

*Yogurt made the traditional way! Most likely, yogurt originated by accident when nomadic tribes traveled the desert. Ask a Hellene about the origins of yogurt, though, and you will hear that the gods of Mount Olympus created this staple of the Greek diet. Greeks enjoy yogurt mixed with honey as a snack, anytime of the day or night. Use it as a sauce over rice or wheat, with dolmathes instead of avgolemono, as an appetizer in tzaziki and even in cakes.*

3 quarts milk
1/2 cup yogurt (starter)

Pour milk in a large pot and bring to boil, stirring so it will not scorch. Watch carefully so milk does not boil over. Remove from heat and cool to lukewarm. If you can hold your little finger in the milk and count to eight, it is cool enough or 115 degrees. Thin your starter with a small amount of the cooled milk and combine with the milk in pot. Cover and allow yogurt pot to set in a warm place (draft-free) several hours or overnight. Cover with a blanket to keep warm.

Strain through several layers of cheesecloth overnight. Remove from bag and place in container and refrigerate. Keeps about one week.

# Yogurt-Garlic Dip (Tzaziki)

*Common throughout the entire Mediterranean region, this recipe evolved to flavor the yogurt with raw garlic and added the cucumber for a refreshing sensation.*

1 32-ounce container plain yogurt
3 cloves garlic
2 cucumbers, peeled and seeded
1 tablespoon olive oil
1 teaspoon dried dill weed
1/4 teaspoon sugar (or more if desired)
salt and pepper to taste

Strain yogurt in a sieve lined with double layers of cheesecloth in refrigerator for several hours or overnight to remove excess liquid. Peel and seed cucumber, salt lightly and let sit for at least 15 minutes. In food processor with metal blade, finely chop garlic, place in a large bowl and add the drained yogurt. With shredding disc, grate the cucumber and squeeze out excess liquid, add to yogurt and garlic mixture. Add remaining ingredients and blend well. Taste for seasoning. Chill until ready to serve.

Can be served as a sauce with meatballs, or as a dip with pita wedges or crackers.

# Garlic Sauce I (Skordalia)

*Garlic lovers will be pleased to know this sauce will guarantee them a seat in theaters and ward off evil. This garlic dip is for boiled and fried shrimp, fried fish (salt cod) and fried or fresh vegetables. Try it atop eggplant or zucchini!*

**I:**
5 to 6 cloves garlic, peeled and chopped
2 to 3 cups of coarse white bread, cubed
1 cup olive oil, to taste
1/2 cup white wine vinegar, to taste
salt and white pepper, to taste

Soak the bread cubes in vinegar for five minutes or until liquid is absorbed. Blend garlic, 1 teaspoon olive oil, and salt in blender or food processor until smooth. Add bread and continue processing while slowly adding the remaining olive oil. Blend until smooth (the consistency of pudding), adding more vinegar or oil for taste. Season with salt and white pepper. Chill overnight before serving.

**Note:** For a change of pace, try substituting two cups of white-bean purée for the bread in this recipe. Adds a different kind of food value!

**II.**
1 medium garlic head, whole
2 1/2 cups homemade mashed potatoes (not instant)
1/3 cup cider vinegar or lemon juice
2 egg yolks
1 1/2 teaspoons salt
1 cup pure olive oil

# Garlic Sauce II (Skordalia)

*A less garlicky version, but equally delicious.*

Clean and mash garlic cloves with the salt in a heavy-bowl until a smooth paste. In a large bowl, beat mashed potatoes with an electric mixer until fluffy. Add garlic paste and continue beating. Add vinegar and egg yolks and blend thoroughly. Continue beating and slowly add the olive oil. Beat until a smooth consistency. Cover and refrigerate before serving. Serve with fried fish, boiled shrimp, fried eggplant or fried zucchini.

> To get back to the "classic" way of preparing the skordalia, you need a wooden mortar and pestle, called a goudi. Pound the garlic with a pestle until thoroughly mashed, adding the bread and potato very gradually until paste-like. Then add the oil and vinegar gradually to proper consistency.

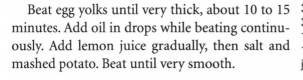
# Greek-style Mayonnaise (Mayoneza)

*Unlike most classic recipes, this one traveled from France to Greece. This fresh mayonnaise can be used on fish, boiled meats and chicken. Can be kept in refrigerator for about a week.*

Beat egg yolks until very thick, about 10 to 15 minutes. Add oil in drops while beating continuously. Add lemon juice gradually, then salt and mashed potato. Beat until very smooth.

3 egg yolks
3/4 cup olive oil
1 teaspoon salt
1 boiled potato, mashed
juice of 1 lemon

# Oil & Oregano Basting Sauce (Lathorigano)

*Where would the Greek cook be without those basics—olive oil and lemon juice!*

Combine above ingredients and use for basting meats, poultry or fish.

1 cup olive oil
1/2 cup lemon juice (fresh)
2 cloves minced garlic
1 tablespoon oregano
salt and pepper

# Savory Tomato Sauce

*Delicious when served over rice pilaf, meatballs, pasta, etc. A good basic tomato sauce.*

2 tablespoons oil
1 small onion, finely chopped
1 large clove garlic, minced
1 large can tomatoes, cut in pieces
1 small can tomato paste
3 tablespoons sugar
1 teaspoon salt, dash of pepper
1 teaspoon oregano
1 teaspoon minced parsley
1/2 cup or more chicken broth

Brown onion and garlic in oil, add tomatoes, tomato paste and seasonings, stirring until smooth. Simmer on low heat; add broth and continue to cook slowly several hours, stirring occasionally. If sauce becomes too thick, thin with additional chicken broth.

# Tomato Sauce (Domata Saltsa)

*For garlic lovers only!*

3 pounds canned tomatoes
  (including the liquid)
1 cup parsley, chopped
3 bay leaves
1 tablespoon dark brown sugar
1/2 cup olive oil
1 1/2 large onions, chopped
1/3 cup garlic, minced
salt to taste

Place all ingredients in a saucepan over medium heat. Simmer gently, stirring occasionally, for 1½ hours until all the liquid has evaporated. As the sauce cooks, most of the garlic aroma disappears.

# Egg-Lemon Sauce (Avgolemono)

*A classic Greek sauce with a prized lemony flavor. Crowns many of our Greek dishes such as dolmathes and tripe soup (patsa). The most important rule is to keep the sauce temperature below 160 degrees to prevent curdling.*

3 eggs separated
juice of 2 lemons (1/3 to 1/2 cup)
1 cup hot broth or stock
1 tablespoon cornstarch

When preparing a dish requiring avgolemono sauce, use the broth in which the dish was cooked. In a medium-size bowl, beat egg whites until stiff. Add egg yolks and continue beating until thick. Slowly add lemon juice beating constantly. Dissolve cornstarch in a little cool water and add to hot broth or stock. Slowly add stock to egg mixture while continuously beating until smooth and creamy. Serve over prepared dish.

## HOME PRESERVED GRAPEVINE LEAVES

Pick young and tender grapevine leaves about the size of the palm of your hand. Wash thoroughly and cut off the stem to the base of the leaf. Arrange the leaves in a stack of eight or ten, dull side down. Roll stack and tie with a string. Continue with all your grapevine leaves. Bring two quarts of water with half a cup of salt to a boil in enamel or stainless kettle. Blanch the rolls for at least two minutes in the boiling brine. Remove to colander then pack as tightly as possible into quart-size canning jars. Cover with boiling brine and seal, or you may use immediately for preparing dolmathes.

If the leaves are to be used immediately, simply blanch and fill as desired.

To freeze, leaves should be washed, stems removed. Blanch in brine for two minutes, drain thoroughly. Separate leaves and dry on paper towels, pack in airtight container and freeze.

Some of our Santa Barbara cooks use nasturtium leaves instead: sprinkle the dolmathes with tasty and pretty nasturtium flowers for a nice touch.

# SOUPS

# Chicken Egg Lemon Soup (Avgolemono)

*A classic in every Greek kitchen. At the first sign of any illness, cooks start boiling chicken for soup, the universal remedy for everything from the common cold to a hangover. Make it rich with bits of chicken added with the pasta or rice if you like. The Greek cook adds eggs and lemon for a very filling and delicious soup. With the pasta you get a very hearty and tasty soup that makes a complete meal with some crusty bread.*

8 cups rich chicken broth
1/2 cup manestra (orzo or rosamarino)
4 eggs
juice of 2 lemons (1/3 cup)

Bring broth to a boil; season to taste. Add manestra and cook until tender, about 20 minutes. Remove from heat.

In a large bowl, beat the eggs until light and frothy; slowly add lemon juice and continue beating until thick. Add broth a little at a time to eggs, mixing slowly. Return to pan and mix well. Serve hot.

**Note:** For a richer soup, instead of 4 whole eggs, substitute 2 whole eggs and 2 (or 3) egg yolks.

To make a rich broth, in a large pot bring to boil enough water to cover either chicken bones, necks, scraps, or whole cut up chicken, with large carrot, scraped but not peeled, one small whole onion with skin left on and ½ cup celery tops with leaves. Simmer for at least one hour, skimming broth and seasoning with salt and pepper to your taste. Discard bones and vegetables and clean off chicken meat to use another time. Strain broth and allow to cool. Discard accumulated fat from cold broth.

If desired, grated raw carrot, grated raw potato and bits of the meat used to make the broth can be added and boiled for 5 minutes after the manestra cooks, before adding the eggs and lemon juice.

# Bean Soup (Fasolada)

*The mainstay of the Greek villages, this hearty soup can be served on a cold and rainy day with crusty bread. Beans have sustained the Hellenes since the Bronze Age.*

2 cups white Navy beans
8 cups water
1/3 cup olive oil
1 medium onion, chopped
1 clove garlic, minced
1 cup chopped celery with leaves
1 cup thinly sliced carrots
2 tablespoons chopped parsley
1 can chopped tomatoes
2 teaspoons salt
1/2 teaspoon pepper

Cover beans with water, bring to boil for 2 minutes, cover with a lid and allow to sit at least 6 hours, or overnight. Drain. In a large soup pot, sauté onion, garlic, celery and carrots until slightly browned. Add tomatoes, parsley and beans, mix well. Add 8 cups water and bring to a boil, stirring occasionally. Cook an hour (or more) until beans are tender, adding more water if necessary to keep the beans covered. When beans are almost done, add the salt and pepper to taste. Serve hot with crusty bread.

# Lentil Soup (Faki Soupa)

*A favorite from the times of the ancient Greeks—their soul food! Lentil soup appears on the Lenten menu several times during the forty-day season!*

Wash lentils and drain. Saute vegetables in olive oil in large soup pot. Add lentils and bay leaf and enough water to cover, stir, bring to boil, reduce heat and simmer for about 45 minutes. Add additional water when necessary to keep lentils covered. When lentils are almost tender, add salt and pepper to taste. Serve hot with a splash of vinegar, if desired.

1 pound lentils
2 medium onions, chopped
3 celery ribs, chopped
1 carrot, thinly sliced
1 clove garlic, minced
1 large bay leaf
2 tablespoons olive oil
salt and pepper to taste
Red wine vinegar, optional

# Greek Easter Soup (Mageritsa)

*The Lenten season in the Orthodox church is observed with fasting for 40 days before Easter. Midnight service at Greek Easter is the most dramatic of all the rituals, ending with the ancient Byzantine chant, "Christ is Risen" (Christos Anesti). The celebration continues with feasting, and to break the Lenten fast, this soup is customarily prepared following the Resurrection Service. Traditionally it is made with lamb heart and lungs, but since it is difficult to find these organ meats in the United States, the lamb shanks and necks are substituted.*

2 pounds lamb shanks or necks
1/2 bunch green onions
1/2 cup chopped celery
1/2 cup chopped parsley
1/4 cup chopped fresh dill weed or
   1 tablespoon dried
3 tablespoons butter
1 cup rice
salt and pepper to taste

**Avgolemono sauce:**
3 eggs
1/3 to 1/2 cup lemon juice

Wash meat thoroughly and place in large pot with water, salt and pepper. Cover and simmer for 1½ hours. Skim froth that forms on broth. Strain broth and skim off fat, refrigerate. Remove meat from bones and chop. In large kettle, sauté onions and celery in butter until lightly browned, add reserved meat, strained broth, parsley and dill. Bring to boil, add rice, cover and simmer for 30 minutes. Adjust seasoning. Remove from heat and prepare avgolemono sauce.

**Avgolemono sauce:** Beat the 3 eggs until frothy, slowly add lemon juice and continue beating. Add 2 cups broth to egg mixture, stirring continuously, return mixture to pot and mix thoroughly and serve immediately.

# Garbanzo Soup (Revithia Soupa)

*One of the basic soups of Greece, especially at the monasteries where additional onion is used to thicken the soup.*

Cover garbanzos with warm water and soak overnight. Drain beans, sprinkle with soda and let stand 30 minutes. Rinse under warm water, then rub with towel to loosen skins. Rinse and place in stockpot. (Note: These steps may be omitted if using canned garbanzos.)

Cover beans with water; bring to boil. Skim if needed. Add oil, onion, lemon juice, salt and pepper to taste; cover and simmer 45 minutes, stirring occasionally. When beans are tender, puree half the beans and return to pot. Add rice and continue cooking until rice is tender, adding more water if necessary. In a small bowl, with a fork beat the tahini with the ½ cup cold water. Take 1 cup of the soup and add it gradually to the tahini mixture. Stir the tahini mixture into the soup pot. Remove from heat and serve warm with additional olive oil and lemon juice over each serving.

1 pound dry garbanzos, washed
2 teaspoons baking soda
1/2 cup olive oil
1 large onion, chopped
1/3 cup fresh lemon juice
1/3 cup rice
1/2 cup tahini
1/2 cup cold water
Salt and pepper to taste

# Yellow Split Pea Purée (Fava)

*Mention split pea soup and you envision a thickened green broth, perhaps with a bit of ham tossed in. The Greek cook takes the yellow split peas and makes a puréed soup thick enough so that you can eat with a scoop from a piece of onion. It's strictly a vegetarian dish; make plenty and use the leftovers to make the fava cakes noted at the end of the recipe.*

1/2 pound yellow split peas
1 small onion, finely chopped
1/4 cup chopped celery
1/2 small clove garlic, minced
olive oil and lemon juice

Wash split peas and combine with remaining ingredients with enough water to cover generously. Bring to boil and simmer until tender. Press through a sieve, or whirl in processor to puree.

Drizzle with olive oil over each serving and a squeeze of lemon. Use a sliver of onion to scoop the soup for added flavor.

**Note:** If you have any leftovers, mix with a small grated onion, ¼ cup chopped parsley, 2 eggs, ⅓ to ½ cup bread crumbs and some grated cheese to taste. Season with salt and pepper, shape into balls or ovals, dip in flour and deep fry until golden.

# Fish Soup (Psarosoupa)

*Light and tasty, a quick and easy soup.*

Clean and wash the fish. Cut into thick slices. Put the water into a saucepan and bring to a boil. Add the vegetables (except potatoes), salt, pepper and oil. Boil for 45 minutes. Reduce heat to simmering point and add the pieces of fish and potatoes. Simmer for 15 minutes. Serves 5 to 6.

2 1/2 to 3 pounds fish
8 cups water
2 large onions, sliced
2 carrots, diced
2 chopped celery stalks
chopped parsley
salt and pepper
1/2 cup olive oil
4 medium-size potatoes, diced

# Tripe Soup (Patsa)

*After a night of partying, a serving of this soup is a "must" for many.*

2 to 3 pounds lamb tripe
2 to 3 cloves garlic, pressed
1 bay leaf
1 small onion, quartered
salt and pepper to taste
egg-lemon sauce

**Avgolemono Sauce:**
3 eggs separated
juice of 2 lemons (1/3 to 1/2 cup)
1 cup broth or stock, hot
1 tablespoon cornstarch

Cut open the tripe and wash thoroughly. Put into saucepan, cover with cold water, add salt, bring to boiling point then drain. Cover generously with fresh water, garlic, onion, bay leaf , salt and pepper and bring again to the boil. Simmer gently until tender, about 2 hours. Drain and reserve liquid. Cut tripe into one-inch pieces, return to pot with the reserved liquid, adding additional water or chicken broth if needed. Simmer for an additional 30 minutes, correct seasoning then prepare the egg-lemon sauce. Serve hot.

**Avgolemono Sauce:** When preparing a dish requiring avgolemono sauce, use the broth in which the dish was cooked. In a medium-size bowl, beat egg whites until stiff. Add egg yolks and continue beating until thick. Slowly add lemon juice beating constantly. Dissolve cornstarch in a little cool water and add to hot broth or stock. Slowly add stock to egg mixture while continuously beating until smooth and creamy. Serve over prepared dish.

# BREADS

# New Year's Bread (Vasilopita)

*This bread is traditionally baked on New Year's Day in honor of St. Basil. To help his needy flock without causing them any embarrassment, he had the bakers insert a gold coin in each loaf of bread to be distributed throughout the parish. We continue this tradition today, and instead of a gold coin, we wrap a coin, in any denomination, with aluminum foil and place in the dough while kneading. When the bread is cut, whoever finds the coin in their piece has good luck for the year.*

Dissolve yeast in warm water. In a large bowl, add the scalded milk, butter, salt, honey and cool to lukewarm. Add the eggs and remaining ingredients except flour and sesame seeds and beat until blended. Add 2 cups of the flour and beat until smooth. With a wooden spoon mix in enough flour to make a smooth dough that can be handled easily. On a floured board, knead gently for about 10 minutes, adding more flour if necessary. Place dough in a greased bowl, turn dough to grease top, cover with a towel, place in a warm place until doubled in bulk. Knead again and allow to rise two more times. This is a rich dough and will take extra time to rise, so don't be impatient.

Divide dough and shape into two large, round loaves and place into greased pans. Let rise until double, brush with egg yolk beaten with a little milk, and sprinkle with sesame seeds. Bake at 375 degrees for 15 minutes, reduce temperature to 325 degrees and continue to bake an additional 20 minutes, or until golden and tests done. Cool on wire racks.

4 cakes compressed yeast (or 4 packages dry yeast)
1/2 cup lukewarm water
2 1/2 pounds flour
1 teaspoon salt
1 1/2 cups scalded milk, cooled
1/2 pound melted butter
grated rind from 1 lemon and 1 orange
2 tablespoons bourbon or brandy
1 tablespoon mahleb (available in the Middle Eastern markets) or substitute ground cardamom seed.
1/2 cup liquid strained from boiled whole allspice (6 berries), 1 stick cinnamon and 6 whole cloves
6 eggs
1 1/2 cups sugar
1/2 cup honey
sesame seeds

# Sweet Easter Bread (Tsoureki)

*A delightful bread, sweet and flavorful. Wonderful when toasted! Traditionally, red-colored Easter eggs are placed atop the loaf before the last rise. Some place four eggs in the sign of the cross, others simply place a single egg in the center.*

1 cup butter
2 cups sugar
2 cups warm milk
3 packages dry yeast
2 tablespoons vegetable oil
6 eggs at room temperature
2 teaspoons vanilla or 1 teaspoon
   crushed mastiha crystals
   (available at Greek specialty
   stores)
2 1/2 pounds unbleached white
   flour
sesame seeds
1 beaten egg

Melt butter; add sugar; stir well and cool to lukewarm. In a large bowl, dissolve yeast in milk. Add warm melted butter mixture; stir in oil, then gradually add eggs, slightly beaten. Add flavorings and blend well. Gradually add flour a little at a time to make a very elastic dough. Knead well, 8 to 10 minutes. Place dough in large bowl, well greased, turning to grease top. Cover with a tea towel and allow to rise until double. May take 3 to 4 hours. Punch down dough and knead again, 3 to 4 minutes. Divide dough into 6 or 8 pieces. Shape into long loaves, braids or desired shape. Place on greased pans and let rise until double, 1 hour or more. Brush tops with 1 egg beaten with a little milk; sprinkle with sesame seeds. Bake on middle rack of 350-degree oven 25 to 30 minutes, until nicely browned. Cool completely on wire racks.

## EASTER EGGS

In every Greek Orthodox household on the Thursday before Easter Sunday, the dyeing of eggs is a ritual. Easter eggs represent the life-giving resurrection of Christ and the promise of everlasting life. The deep red color recalls the blood Christ shed on the cross. It is customary to greet one another with the words "Christos Anesti" (Christ is Risen) and to reply "Alethos Anesti" (Truly, He is Risen) while striking the pointed ends of the eggs together. Good fortune is promised to the one whose egg remains uncracked. This cracking of the eggs symbolizes Christ's resurrection.

**eggs   red food coloring   1/2 cup white vinegar   1 teaspoon salt   Oil**

Cover eggs with warm water for 15 minutes, remove carefully and dry each egg. Fill a stainless steel or enameled saucepan with fresh water, enough to cover eggs when they are added. Dissolve food coloring in a little hot water; stir in vinegar and salt. Add to water and slowly bring to a boil and simmer about 5 minutes. Remove from heat; slowly add as many eggs into water as will fit in one layer. Add additional hot water if necessary to cover eggs. Return to heat and simmer, uncovered, 30 minutes. Remove eggs carefully and wipe dry. Polish with an oiled cloth until they shine.

# Ceremonial Bread (Artoklasia Artos)

*There is a service in the Greek Orthodox Church called the Artoklasia Service, dating back to the times of the Apostles. It commemorates Christ's miracle of feeding the multitudes when He blessed the five loaves and two fishes, feeding over 5,000 people (Luke 9:15) on the seashore of Galilee.*

12 eggs, beaten
10 pounds flour
1 1/2 pounds butter or margarine, melted
2 1/2 cups sugar
4 to 6 packages yeast
grated rind of 2 oranges
1/4 cup cognac
1 teaspoon anise seed (rolled flat)
1 1/2 quarts warm milk
1 cup warm water
1 teaspoon salt

Place flour in large bowl. Dissolve yeast in 1 cup warm water; add to flour. Add eggs, butter and sugar and slowly add warm milk mixed with water. (May take more milk) Mix well. Add rind, cognac, anise seed and salt. Knead until dough is soft and smooth. Cover and put in a warm place to double in size. Press down gently and let rise again. Divide dough into 5 pieces and put into five greased 9-inch round pans. Cover; let rise until double in size. (If all bread cannot be baked at the same time, cover only those that will be baked first to slow down the rising process.)

Bake at 375 degrees for 15 minutes, then lower temperature to 350 degrees and continue baking for 45 minutes longer. Remove from oven and brush with a mixture of ½ cup honey which has been diluted with 2 tablespoons warm water. Sprinkle with powdered sugar.

## THE ARTOKLASIA SERVICE

This service is a gesture of thanksgiving for God's blessings. Artoklasia takes place after the liturgy, on any Sunday decided upon by the family wishing to secure blessings and prayers for well being of a relative, friend, church-related organization, etc. Five loaves of bread, a small container of olive oil and a small container of wine are brought to church, blessed in a short service of blessings and prayers for health and prosperity and then distributed to the congregation.

# Altar Bread (Prosphoron)

*The women of the church prayerfully prepare the round loaf of leavened bread used in the preparation of the gifts of Holy Communion; it is called prosphoron, meaning offering, that is "the bread of offering."*

5 cups flour, sifted
2 1/4 cups warm water
1 envelope yeast
1 teaspoon salt
Religious seal *(Sfragitha)*

## THE PROSPHORON SEAL

The seal on the top surface is a carved, wooden piece with the following diagram:

The Greek letters IC and XC are abbreviations for the words Jesus Christ. NIKA means conquers. The large triangular piece represents the Virgin Mary. The smaller triangles, the Angelic Hosts and the Saints of the Orthodox Church. The bread is cut by the priest in preparation of the Holy Communion and the remaining bread is distributed to the faithful after the service.

Dissolve yeast in warm water. Add sifted flour and salt and knead until smooth. Place in bowl, cover and let rise. When double in size, knead again. Divide dough in half and place in floured cake pans. Do not grease pans. Dip seal in flour and stamp each bread forcefully. Let rise and bake for about 30 minutes at 375 degrees.

**Note:** Without the religious stamp, this is an excellent everyday bread recipe. Any, or all, of the following make tasty additions to the bread (add to the yeast and water when adding the flour and salt, before kneading): chopped Kalamata olives, rosemary, oregano, sun-dried tomatoes, garlic. This bread is wonderful when sliced while still warm from the oven and simply topped with butter!

To make everyday bread, bake the dough in loaf pans. Double the recipe to make three loaves of bread.

# Ceremonial Wheat (Kolyva)

*Kolyva represents one of the many traditions continued for hundreds of years among Greek Orthodox people. The kolyva symbolizes resurrection. As St. John said, "Unless a grain of wheat falls into earth and dies, it remains alone; but if it dies, it bears much fruit." (John 12:24)*

In large canning kettle, cover wheat generously with cold water and allow to stand overnight. Drain and cover with fresh water. Cook about 4 hours, or until tender, stirring often with wooden spoon to prevent sticking. Drain and spread on a large cloth to absorb excess moisture. Brown sesame seeds and crumbs separately in moderate oven, stirring often. Prepare a serving tray edged with paper doilies and lined with waxed paper. Mix wheat with all ingredients except powdered sugar, dragees and almonds. Place mixture on tray and mound slightly with palms of hands. Sift powdered sugar generously over wheat to cover entirely. Press down firmly with waxed paper to make a smooth, compact top. Make an impression of a large cross in the sugar and fill with silver dragees. On either side of cross form initials of deceased using ground cinnamon. Make a border at edge of tray with almonds.

5 pounds whole wheat kernels
1 1/2 pounds sesame seeds
2 cups Zwieback crumbs
4 cups chopped walnuts
2 1/2 cups granulated sugar
4 teaspoons cinnamon
1 teaspoon nutmeg
1/2 cup chopped parsley
3 boxes currants
seeds of one pomegranate (if available)
1 box powdered sugar
3 ounces silver dragees
blanched almonds

## THE MEMORIAL SERVICE

The ancient Greeks brought this special food to honor the dead on All Soul's Day and the Orthodox Church continues this custom by including it in their special memorial service for departed souls. The boiled wheat grain symbolizes resurrection and is traditionally offered forty days after death and in following years after a memorial service. Even though the Kolyva is quite delicious, it is prepared only to remember the dead; it is not served at any other time, only when it is distributed among the parishioners following the service.

# Greek Sesame Bread (Kouloura)

*This traditional bread with sesame seeds on top is baked in every Greek kitchen.*

2 packages dry yeast (or fresh)
1/2 cup warm water
2 cups warm milk
3 tablespoons sugar
3 tablespoons butter or oil
3/4 teaspoon salt
7 cups all-purpose flour
1 egg
1 egg yolk
1/4 cup sesame seeds

Place yeast in warm water with a pinch of sugar. Scald milk, add sugar, butter and salt and place in large mixing bowl. Add dissolved yeast and egg and enough of the flour to make a soft dough that does not stick to the hands. Knead until dough is smooth and elastic, adding more flour a little at a time, if necessary. Place in a greased bowl, cover with towel and set aside to rise until doubled in bulk.

Punch down dough and divide into two and allow to rest 15 minutes. Shape into long rope, make a circle and place in greased, round baking pan. Allow to rise about 1 hour, until doubled. Brush top with egg yolk and sprinkle generously with the sesame seeds. Bake in preheated oven at 375 degrees for 45 minutes. Remove from oven, allow to cool 10 minutes then remove from pan.

# Braided Bread

*A dressed-up version of a simple white bread.*

Melt butter and allow to cool. Combine water, sugar, ginger and yeast in a small bowl. Cover and let stand in a warm place until it rises with froth, and bubbles. Takes about 10 minutes.

1/4 cup butter or margarine
1/2 cup warm water
2 packages dry yeast
1 teaspoon sugar
1/4 teaspoon ginger

Sift together dry ingredients into a large bowl. Add warm water and blend by hand. Add yeast mixture and blend.

2 cups flour
1/2 cup dried skim milk
1/2 cup sugar
1 cup warm water

Add salt, eggs, flour and the melted butter to the above mixture. Stir to blend. Place dough on floured surface and knead thoroughly using more flour as needed (about 1 cup). Lightly oil a large pan and place dough on it; cover with waxed paper and towel and let rise in a warm place for 1¼ hours. Punch down lightly. Divide dough into thirds, and each piece into thirds again. Roll each piece into a rope 8 to 10 inches long. Using 3 ropes, proceed to braid the dough pinching the ends to secure the dough. Place on greased cookie sheet. Cover and allow to rise for one half hour. With a fork, beat one egg yolk with 2 teaspoons water. Brush on braids and sprinkle with sesame or poppy seeds. Bake at 350 degrees for about 30 minutes.

1 teaspoon salt
2 eggs, well beaten
3 cups flour

Makes 3 braided loaves. Recipe can be doubled. If shaped into rolls, single recipe will yield 2 dozen rolls.

# Cheese-filled Rolls (Kallitsounia)

*A recipe originating on Crete—these rolls are delicious when served with morning or afternoon coffee.*

**Dough:**
1 package dry yeast
1/4 cup warm water
1 cup warm milk
1/4 cup sugar
2 eggs, beaten
1/2 cup melted butter
1/2 teaspoon salt
3 cups flour

**Filling:**
8 ounces ricotta cheese
8 ounces feta cheese
8 ounces kasseri cheese
1 egg
2 tablespoons sugar

Soften yeast in warm water. In large bowl pour warm milk, add sugar and salt. Stir in yeast, eggs, butter hand beat well. Gradually add enough flour until batter is soft and spongy. Batter will be sticky. Set aside and prepare cheese mixture. In food processor, if available, combine the cheeses. Add the egg and sugar and blend well.

Coat a frying pan with oil and heat over medium flame. Have a saucer nearby with oil in it to dip your fingers. This will keep the dough from sticking to your hands. Pinch a ball of dough (about 2 tablespoons), press slightly and place 1 teaspoon of cheese filling in it and reshape the dough to enclose filling. Flatten it out and fry, about 1 minute each side. Drain on paper towel. To serve, sprinkle with powdered sugar, or drizzle with honey, if preferred. Serve warm. May be reheated in a warm oven or low microwave oven before sprinkling with the sugar or honey.

# Rolled Cheese-filled Buns

*Another variation of the cheese turnover.*

Combine the liquid ingredients until well blended. Add enough flour to make a soft dough. Set aside and prepare cheese filling. On a floured surface, roll out the dough to about ¼ inch thickness. Cut into rounds with a saucer, place a generous spoonful of filling on half the round, fold over and seal edges with the tines of a fork. Deep fry until golden, drain on paper towel and serve with a drizzle of honey.

**Dough:**
2 eggs, beaten
1/2 cup oil
1/4 teaspoon lemon juice
1 cup milk
5 cups flour
1 teaspoon baking soda
dash salt

**Filling:**
Prepare filling according to previous recipe.

# Cheese Muffins

*Make these muffins to serve with a hearty soup or casserole.*

1 egg
1/2 cup milk
3/4 cup grated Romano cheese
1 cup flour
3 teaspoons baking powder
2 tablespoons soft butter or
    margarine

Beat egg and milk together. Add sifted dry ingredients and cheese. Add butter. Fill greased muffin cups ¾ full. Bake at 400 degrees for 15 minutes. Makes 12.

# SALADS

# Village Salad (Horiatiki Salata)

*In a small country village near the mountains, the priest's wife suddenly was told that her in-laws were coming to visit. At that time there was nothing in the house to prepare for a meal. She went out to the vegetable garden to pick all kinds of vegetables and green herbs. Then she walked to the shepherd's home where she got some cheese. Then she went to the olive grove where the owner had cured olives. She always had olive oil at home. When she got back she threw all those goodies in a bowl, tossed them and there was the horiatiki salata ready for the in-laws!*

The classic Greek salad! These fresh ingredients are found in the backyard garden and of every Greek cook.

Toss together all ingredients except feta cheese. Sprinkle cheese over salad and serve.

tomatoes, chilled and cut in large pieces
cucumbers, peeled and sliced
green onions, thinly sliced
green pepper, thinly sliced
olive oil
Greek olives (black)
oregano
salt
feta cheese, crumbled

---

## BASIC OLIVE-OIL DRESSINGS

### OLIVE OIL AND LEMON JUICE

2 parts extra-virgin olive oil
1 part fresh lemon juice
Salt and pepper
Herbs (any of the following: oregano, thyme, dill, marjoram)

Mix together the olive oil and lemon juice in a small jar. Add the salt, pepper, and herbs. Shake to mix together.

### OLIVE OIL AND VINEGAR

2 parts extra-virgin olive oil
1 part red wine vinegar
Salt and pepper
Herbs (any of the following: oregano, thyme, dill, and marjoram)

Mix together the olive oil and vinegar in a small jar. Add the salt, pepper, and herbs. Shake to mix together.

# Tomato Salad with Feta (Domatosalata)

*On a hot summer day, there is nothing more inviting than this easy to prepare salad famous in villages and especially in Santorini, known for the sweetest tomatoes in Greece produced from the rich volcanic soil. The best time to make this salad is when vine-ripened tomatoes are in season.*

3 tablespoons olive oil
1/4 teaspoon oregano
salt and pepper
1/2 cup feta cheese, crumbled
1 pound firm, ripe tomatoes

In a small bowl combine the oil, oregano, salt and pepper with a fork. Let stand. When ready to serve, slice the tomatoes and place on a platter, drizzle the dressing over the tomatoes then sprinkle generously with the feta cheese.

# Athenian Salad

*Strictly a city dish! If you sit down for a meal in the Plaka in Athens, you will most certainly be served this salad. In Greece, a meal without a salad is no meal at all.*

variety of greens (lettuce, Swiss
    chard, escarole, endive)
chopped celery
green onions, sliced thin
cucumbers, peeled and sliced
tomato wedges
green pepper, chopped
anchovies (optional)
feta cheese, cubed
Greek olives (black)

Dressing: Use two parts olive oil, one part wine vinegar or lemon juice. Add salt, pepper and oregano. Toss and serve.

# Eggplant Salad (Melitzanosalata)

*Everyone is familiar with the classic Greek main dish, moussaka. But eggplant lovers should try this cool eggplant salad for a nice change of pace.*

Bake whole eggplants in moderate oven for about 1 hour. Remove from oven, dip into cold water and peel. Dice the pulp and place in salad bowl previously rubbed with garlic. Add remaining ingredients and mix well with wooden spoon. Allow to marinate before serving.

This salad is delicious served with meat or fish.

4 small eggplants or 2 large round ones
3 tomatoes cut into small pieces
2 tablespoons chopped parsley
1 small onion, grated
1 cup olive oil
3 tablespoons vinegar (or wine vinegar)
salt and pepper to taste
1 clove garlic

# Hot Potato Salad (Patatosalata)

*A common family dish. Serve with sliced tomatoes and cubes of feta on the side.*

Boil potatoes in their skins until tender. Drain and peel. Cut in quarters and then in halves. Mix all ingredients together and pour over warm potatoes. Toss lightly, garnish with parsley. Serve warm or at room temperature. Serves 6.

4 large potatoes
1/2 cup olive oil
1/4 cup vinegar or lemon juice
1 teaspoon oregano
1 tablespoon minced parsley as garnish
1/4 cup finely chopped green onions
salt and pepper

# Pasta Salad

*Take traditional Greek ingredients and use them with a pasta mixture for a tasty and delicious salad.*

12 ounces uncooked rotini or
　rotelle pasta
1/2 cup red wine vinegar
1/2 cup olive oil
1/2 cup minced fresh parsley
1/4 cup minced fresh mint
2 tablespoons dried oregano
2 teaspoons dried thyme
1/2 teaspoon salt
1 teaspoon pepper
15-ounce can garbanzo beans,
　drained and rinsed
4 plum tomatoes, diced
4 to 6 scallions, diced
8 ounces feta cheese, crumbled
I cup pitted, coarsely chopped
　Kalamata olives (optional)

Cook pasta in boiling water until al dente, 9 to 11 minutes. Drain.

In large bowl, stir together vinegar, oil, parsley, mint, oregano, thyme, salt, and pepper. Add cooked pasta, beans, tomatoes, scallions, and cheese, mix well. Chill at least 1 hour before serving. Serves 6 to 8.

# Mediterranean Barley Salad

*This salad has a lot of substance, enhanced with a tangy dressing and colorful chopped vegetables.*

Place barley, water, and salt in saucepan and bring to boil. Cover and reduce heat and simmer 45 minutes or until barley is tender and liquid is absorbed.

Combine olive oil, lemon juice, vinegar and oregano. Mix well and pour over cooked barley. Cool to room temperature then gently stir in tomatoes, peppers, feta and parsley, in that order. Serve chilled or at room temperature.

1 cup barley
3 cups water
1 teaspoon salt
1/2 cup olive oil
3 tablespoons lemon juice
3 tablespoons wine vinegar
1 teaspoon oregano
1/3 cup fresh chopped parsley
2 medium tomatoes, peeled and diced
1 sweet red or yellow pepper, peeled and diced
1/2 cup feta cheese, crumbled

# Boiled Greens with Lemon & Olive Oil
# (Horta Vrasta Lathera)

*A sure first sign of spring was black-clothed grandmothers picking young greens on any hillside. The original farmer's market! They would dig them up by the roots. Very delicious!*

3 to 4 bunches dandelions, curly endive, escarole, mustard greens, spinach, Swiss chard, etc.
1/4 cup olive oil
juice of one whole lemon
salt and pepper to taste
crumbled feta (if desired)

Clean and wash thoroughly and drain greens. Cook greens in a large amount of water with salt at a high boil, uncovered, until tender. Drain and place in bowl. Season with olive oil and lemon juice or more if desired.

For a special treat sprinkle with crumbled feta and serve with fresh baked bread. The greens can be served warm or cold. Serves 4.

# SEAFOOD

# Marinated Fish (Marinata)

*A favorite method of preparing fish so that it will keep for days—should there be any left over.*

Cut washed filets into serving pieces, sprinkle with salt and lemon juice. Let stand at least 15 minutes. Roll in flour and fry in hot oil until golden brown on both sides. Remove to a deep platter.

When all fish is fried, strain the oil of burned flour. Return oil to pan. Add the garlic and brown slightly. Add remaining ingredients and bring to boil. Remove from heat and quickly pour over fish. Serve hot or let cool and refrigerate to serve cold.

**Note:** Will keep up to 5 days.

3 pounds fish filets, preferably sea bass
salt and lemon juice
oil for frying
1/2 cup vinegar
3 cloves chopped garlic
1 teaspoon rosemary leaves
1 large bay leaf

# Fried Salted Codfish with Garlic Sauce (Bakaliaros Me Skordalia)

*Salted cod is often the only kind of fish available in inland areas with limited access to fresh fish. This dried cod must be soaked before use in this recipe—it is considered a special treat by many Greeks.*

Cut codfish into squares, wash thoroughly and soak in cold water overnight. The following day, rinse fish several times and allow to drain. When dry, dip in a light batter of flour and milk and fry in hot oil until golden brown. Serve with Garlic Sauce (recipe on page 28).

# Baked Fish (Psari Psito)

*For those who live close to the sea and have access to whole fresh fish, a simple and delicious way to prepare it.*

one whole fish, approximately 3 pounds
1/2 cup olive oil
1/2 cup lemon juice or white wine
1 teaspoon salt
1/8 teaspoon pepper
1/4 teaspoon favorite herb
(i.e. rosemary, thyme, tarragon, parsley)

Rinse fish and lay full length in a shallow pan. Mix remaining ingredients and spoon over the fish. Let stand, refrigerated, for 30 minutes, then turn over and marinate fish an additional 30 minutes. Spoon off some of the marinade to use for basting during baking. Bake at 375 degrees about 25 minutes, or 10 minutes per pound. Baste frequently. Serve whole.

# Baked Fish (Plaki)

*An aromatic variation from the Cyclades*

Pour ¼ cup of the olive oil and the wine in bottom of a baking dish and arrange fish. Sprinkle with lemon juice, half the salt half the pepper, and bake at 350 degrees about 10 minutes.

Wash and cut the spinach and drain. In a casserole boil 4 cups of water. Place spinach and cook for 2 minutes. Drain all water and let spinach to dry.

In a skillet heat the remaining oil, add green onions and regular onions and saute until slightly brown. Add spinach and the rest of the vegetables and cook for 3 minutes, then add tomatoes, currants, remaining salt and pepper, and cook for 10 minutes.

Remove fish from oven and cover with the vegetables. Return to oven and bake 30 minutes or until vegetables and fish are tender. If sauce is thin, spoon out one cup, blend two tablespoons of flour and return to pan. Bake an additional 10 minutes until sauce thickens. Serve with rice pilaf. Serves 6.

2 pounds fish filets (red snapper or orange roughy)
1/2 cup olive oil
1/4 cup dry white wine
1/3 cup lemon juice
2 teaspoons salt
1/2 teaspoon pepper
1 pound fresh spinach
1 cup green onions, chopped
2 large onions, chopped
1/2 cup fresh parsley, chopped
1/2 cup fresh mint, chopped
1/2 cup fresh anise, chopped
2 cups canned tomatoes
1/2 cup black currants

# Baked Fish with Vegetables (Dodecanese-style Plaki)

*This traditional island dish improves in flavor if made the day before and heated through before serving.*

2 to 3 pounds fish filets, preferably red snapper (thin filets not suitable)
1 lemon
wine vinegar
2 tablespoons olive oil
3 to 4 cloves garlic, sliced
2 large onions, thinly sliced
3 celery stalks, chopped
1 green pepper, chopped
1/4 cup parsley, chopped
1 large can tomatoes
salt and pepper
1 bay leaf

Wash filets and place in glass container. Sprinkle with the juice of one lemon and a little vinegar.

Prepare vegetables as follows: In hot olive oil, saute all vegetables, except tomatoes, for about 5 minutes. Mash the tomatoes and add to vegetables along with the juice, and simmer for about 20 minutes, until vegetables are tender. Season with salt, pepper and bay leaf.

Arrange the fish in a baking dish, pour over it the lemon juice marinade and the vegetables. Bake in 375 degree oven for about 30 minutes, or until fish flakes easily. Serves 6

# Pan-fried Fish, Greek-style

*The best way to cook the freshest fish.*

1 pound fish filets (sole, snapper or white fish)
butter
salt, pepper
lemon wedges

Select fresh fish filets, lightly flour. Melt butter in nonstick sauté pan. Place fish in pan and brown on both sides. Reduce heat till cooked through. Squeeze with lemon wedges and serve immediately.

# Fish Salad Mayonnaise (Mayoneza)

*Do not be fooled by the name. This delicious seafood salad is a great way to use leftover fish. It makes for a tasty light lunch.*

Poach the filets in a mixture of water with ¼ cup vinegar, one bay leaf, slice of onion, some celery leaves, salt, pepper, and a squeeze of lemon. When fish flakes easily, remove from liquid and let cool. When cool enough to handle, clean thoroughly and flake into a large bowl. You should have at least 2 cups fish. Clean the boiled potatoes, dice and add to the fish. Add the parsley, onion, celery, relish and enough mayonnaise to bind the mixture. Season with additional salt and pepper, if needed, and the horseradish, if desired. Arrange on a serving platter and chill thoroughly. When ready to serve, garnish with additional parsley and paprika.

2 pounds fish filets (any kind)
poaching liquid
2 large potatoes, boiled
1/2 cup chopped parsley
1/2 cup chopped green onion
1/2 cup chopped celery
2 tablespoons pickle relish
2 tablespoons horseradish
  (optional)
salt and pepper
paprika
mayonnaise

# Fish in Tomato Sauce

*This is also a good way to use leftover fried fish.*

2 to 3 pounds fish filets
flour
3/4 cup olive oil
1/2 cup flour
2 tablespoons red wine vinegar
2 teaspoons tomato paste
1 1/2 cups water
1/2 teaspoon sugar
2 cloves garlic, minced
2 bay leaves
1/8 teaspoon each basil, rosemary,
    tarragon
salt and pepper

Heat oil in skillet. Dredge fish in flour and fry until golden. Remove from skillet and blend in the ½ cup flour then slowly add the remaining ingredients. Simmer for 10 minutes, add fish and heat through. The flavors blend better if prepared the day before.

# Fried Smelts (Marithes Tiganites)

*Greeks wax rhapsodic about these tiny fish. Try a platterful served with salad and cold beer on a hot day. Pretend you're in a seaside taverna overlooking the blue Aegean.*

2 pounds smelts
3/4 cup lemon juice
oregano
salt and pepper
1 cup flour
1/2 cup olive oil
lemon wedges

Clean smelts leaving heads and tails intact and drain. Place in shallow dish, sprinkle with ½ cup lemon juice, oregano, salt and pepper. Dredge smelts in flour shaking off excess and fry quickly in hot olive oil about 1 minute on each side, or until lightly browned. Drain, transfer to heated platter and sprinkle with additional ¼ cup lemon juice and oregano. Garnish with lemon wedges.

# Baked Prawns with Feta

*A delightfully different way to serve shrimp—plentiful in Greece and in Santa Barbara.*

Sauté onion in oil, add green onions and garlic and cook until lightly brown. Add tomatoes, wine, 3 tablespoons of the parsley, oregano, mint, basil, salt and pepper. Cover and simmer 30 minutes. Remove 1 cup of the liquid to dissolve the flour, then return to pan and mix well.

Spoon half the sauce in 9×13-inch baking dish, place the prawns over the sauce and cover with remaining sauce. Sprinkle with feta cheese. Bake in a very hot oven at 400 degrees 10 to 15 minutes or until prawns are pink and feta is melted and lightly brown on top. Remove from oven and sprinkle with remaining parsley. Serve immediately.

2 pounds prawns, precooked and cleaned
1 onion, chopped
1/2 cup olive oil
1 cup chopped green onions
2 cloves garlic, chopped
2 cups canned tomatoes, chopped and drained
1/2 cup dry white wine
1/4 cup parsley, chopped
1/2 teaspoon oregano
1/4 teaspoon salt
1/4 teaspoon pepper
1/2 cup feta cheese crumbled
1/4 teaspoon basil
1/4 cup fresh mint, chopped
2 tablespoons flour

# Caviar Cakes (Tarama Keftedes)

*Resembling crab cakes, an excellent Lenten dish.*

Combine first nine ingredients with ¼ cup olive oil until well mixed. Heat remaining olive oil in skillet. Shape mixture into small cakes, dust with flour and fry in hot oil until nicely browned. Remove to platter. Sprinkle with additional lemon juice and serve warm. Makes about 20 patties.

1 1/2 cups tarama
2 1/2 cups mashed potatoes
1 large onion, grated
1/2 cup chopped parsley
1/2 cup chopped mint
1/4 cup chopped fresh dill weed (1 tablespoon dried)
dash pepper
1/4 cup lemon juice
2 tablespoons vinegar
3/4 cup olive oil
flour

# Baked Stuffed Squid (Kalamaria Yemista)

*This is a time-consuming recipe, but if you love squid—and those who will eat it—it's worth the effort.*

12 squid (4 to 5 inches long)
1 cup chopped onions
2 tablespoons chopped parsley
1/2 cup olive oil
1/2 cup boiled rice
2 tablespoons tomato paste
2 tablespoons chopped mint
salt and pepper

**Sauce:**
3 tablespoons olive oil
1/2 cup white wine
3 to 4 tablespoons water

Wash squid thoroughly removing heads, bones and ink sacs and pulling out the black skin. Wash well and sprinkle with a little salt. Sauté onions in olive oil with parsley and mint until onion is golden brown. Add rice, tomato paste and season with salt and pepper to taste. Cook together a few minutes then set aside to cool. Stuff each squid with above mixture and arrange side by side in oiled baking pan. Mix the sauce ingredients and pour over the squid. Bake at 350 degrees about 1 hour.

# Fried Squid (Kalamarakia Tiganita)

*A typical and favorite seaside treat. Tiny squid, lightly breaded and deep fried.*

2 pounds small squid
oil
2 cups flour
1 teaspoon garlic powder
1 teaspoon salt
1/4 teaspoon pepper
1 teaspoon oregano

Wash squid thoroughly removing heads, bones and ink sacs and pulling out the black skin.. Drain and cut in 1 inch rings. Combine dry ingredients in shallow plate. Pour enough oil in skillet to ½ inch depth. Heat until drop of water sizzles in oil. Dip squid in flour, shake off excess and fry until golden, about 1 to 2 minutes. Drain on paper towels and serve with lemon wedges and garlic sauce or tzatziki.

# Shrimp Pilafi

*A popular Lenten dish—simple, fast, and delicious.*

Wash shrimp and boil in 4 cups salted water for 10 minutes. Remove shrimp to cool. Reserve broth. In a heavy pan or Dutch oven, saute onion with oil. Add tomato sauce, salt and pepper and stir. Add ¼ cup wine and 3 cups of shrimp broth. Bring to a boil and add rice. Stir again and cover. When rice is nearly done, add shrimp. Simmer uncovered until liquid is absorbed. Remove from heat and cover. Let stand for 5 minutes before serving. Sprinkle with parsley and lemon juice, if desired.

2 pounds cooked shrimp
1 medium onion, chopped
1/4 cup vegetable oil or olive oil
2 tablespoons chopped fresh
   parsley
4 ounces tomato sauce
salt and pepper to,taste
1/4 cup white wine
1 cup converted rice
lemon juice (optional)

# Island Shrimp Pilafi with Tomatoes

*A feast for the eye as well as the palate! The addition of bell pepper and brown rice gives this version of shrimp pilaf a distinctly unique taste.*

1 pound cooked shrimp
1 medium onion, chopped
1/3 cup olive oil
8 ounces tomato sauce
1 can peeled, diced tomatoes
  (14 ounce)
1 bell pepper, red, yellow, or green,
  peeled and cut in strips
1 cup converted rice or California
  brown rice
2 cups water
3 tablespoons chopped fresh
  parsley

In a heavy pan or Dutch oven, sauté onion in 2 tablespoons of oil. Add tomato sauce, tomatoes, pepper, water and seasonings. Bring to a boil, add rice, stir and cover. Reduce heat to low and cook for 20 minutes or till almost done (if using brown rice, cook 40 minutes and check liquid, so as not to dry out or burn). Add the shrimp and remaining oil and continue to cook until heated through. Remove from heat and stir in fresh parsley. Serve warm.

If using raw shrimp, clean and de-vein and add to rice mixture at least 5 minutes before finished cooking, until shrimp turns pink.

**Note:** Use long-grain California Jasmine rice for a lighter, more distinctive rice flavor.

# Scallops with Rice (Ktenia Me Rizi)

*With the easy availability of scallops in Santa Barbara, this pilaf variation is popular. Use frozen scallops for extra convenience.*

Sauté onion in butter. Add washed scallops to onion mixture and simmer 15 minutes, turning occasionally. Reserve the liquid from the mixture and set aside both.

Brown the rice in olive oil until golden and place in a 2-quart casserole. In a measuring cup, combine liquid from scallops, wine, salt, and enough water to make 2½ cups. Pour liquid over rice, cover and bake at 400 degrees for 20 minutes. Stir in scallop mixture and bake an additional 10 minutes. Sprinkle with parsley.

1 large onion, chopped
1/2 cup butter
2 pounds scallops
2 tablespoons olive oil
1 cup uncooked rice
1/4 cup white wine
1 teaspoon salt
chopped parsley

# Cold Fish Platter (Senagreda Krea)

*The dramatic presentation is only half the beauty of this recipe; the taste is the other half. A wonderful make-ahead dish for your special buffet table.*

1 whole red snapper, about 6
   pounds
1 onion, chopped
1 carrot, chopped
1 stalk celery, chopped
2 sprigs parsley
2 bay leaves
1/4 cup dry white wine
1/4 cup oil
1 cup water
1 1/2 cups Greek-style
   mayonnaise*
juice of 1 lemon
1/4 cup chopped parsley
salt and pepper to taste
sliced cooked beets
sliced cucumbers
Greek olives

*See *Mayoneza* recipe, page 29

Wash fish well. Sprinkle with salt, pepper and lemon juice. Let stand 30 minutes. Combine onion, carrot, celery, parsley, bay leaves, wine, oil and water in a shallow pan large enough to take the whole fish. Place the fish in pan and cover. Simmer 20 minutes or until fish flakes easily. Do not overcook. Remove fish carefully to a bread board and let cool. Clean fish and reassemble attractively on serving platter. Chill well before covering with the mayonnaise.

When ready to serve, completely cover the fish with mayonnaise. Garnish with the chopped parsley, beets, cucumbers and olives. Serves about 12.

# POULTRY

# Spiced Chicken (Kota Kapama)

*The taste of cinnamon evokes the flavors of the Middle East in this spicy chicken dish for family or friends.*

Sprinkle chicken with salt, pepper and dash cinnamon. In heavy skillet or Dutch oven, brown chicken in butter until golden. Add onions and garlic and brown slightly. In a blender jar, combine the tomatoes, tomato paste, sugar and water and blend until smooth. Pour over chicken. Add cinnamon sticks, cover and simmer until chicken is done; 45 minutes to 1 hour. Remove cinnamon sticks. Arrange chicken on platter. Serve sauce separately with rice, spaghetti or potatoes. Garnish with grated cheese.

1 chicken (3 to 4 pounds) cut into serving pieces
salt, pepper and dash cinnamon
6 tablespoons butter
3 onions, chopped fine
3 cloves garlic, minced (optional)
2 cups canned tomatoes
1 can tomato paste
1 teaspoon sugar
3/4 cup water
2 cinnamon sticks

# Baked Chicken Oregano (Kota Riganato)

*The most basic and classic way to prepare chicken. Always a favorite, you do not have to worry about leftovers!*

3 to 4 pounds chicken parts
juice of 1 lemon
1 teaspoon dried oregano leaves
2 tablespoons olive oil
2 tablespoons melted butter
salt and pepper to taste

Wash chicken parts and drain. Place in buttered, shallow baking pan. Combine remaining ingredients and brush chicken generously, using it all. Bake at 350 degrees for about 1 hour, basting occasionally with pan juices.

An excellent variation of Chicken Riganato is to add potatoes, cut in eighths to the baking pan. Season the potatoes as you would the chicken. The dish may need additional baking time until potatoes are tender.

# Chicken Velvet in Filo Rolls

*This makes a wonderful buffet dish. An easy way to serve chicken, dressed up, and already portioned. Complete the dish with rice pilaf and a tasty, colorful salad.*

In covered skillet cook celery and onion until tender in 1-tablespoon butter. Add chicken with 1 cup Béchamel sauce, parsley and seasonings. Remove from heat and cool for about 1 minute.

To make chicken roll, lay 1 sheet of filo on smooth surface and brush with melted butter. In center of sheet, place ½ sheet filo and brush with butter. Place about ⅓ cup chicken mixture along short end of filo in center about 1 inch from edge. Turn filo over 2 or 3 times to cover filling, fold in sides to enclose filling and roll jelly-roll fashion to end. Brush top with melted butter and lay on ungreased cookie sheet. Continue with filo and filling until all filling is used. You should have about 10 chicken rolls. Bake rolls at 350 degrees for 30 to 40 minutes, until lightly browned and crisp.

**Bechamel Sauce:** Melt butter, stir in flour and salt. Add broth and wine and cook stirring constantly until mixture is thick and bubbly. Combine egg yolks with lemon juice. Stir half the hot mixture into egg, return to saucepan and cook for 2 more minutes, stirring constantly. Makes 3 cups sauce. Mix 1 cup into chicken mixture and serve remaining sauce with chicken rolls.

**Note:** Can be baked in a 9×13-inch pan using ½ pound filo dough. Line pan with 6 sheets buttered filo, spread chicken mixture over filo and top with additional sheets of buttered filo. Score the top and bake at 350 degrees for 50 to 60 minutes. When ready to serve, cut through to bottom crust and serve with sauce.

1 pound filo dough
1/2 teaspoon salt
1 cup chopped celery
1/2 teaspoon nutmeg
1/2 cup chopped onion
1/8 teaspoon pepper
1 tablespoon butter
1 stick melted butter for filo
2 1/2 cups cooked chicken chopped (about 8 boneless breasts)
1 teaspoon dried parsley flakes (or 1 tablespoon fresh)

**Béchamel Sauce:**
6 tablespoons flour
3 cups chicken broth
6 tablespoons butter
1/2 cup white wine
1/2 teaspoon salt
4 egg yolks
3 tablespoons lemon juice

# Yogurt Chicken with Walnuts

*The combination of walnuts and yogurt make a very tender and delicious dish. Perfect for guests!*

4 large chicken breasts
1/4 cup flour
1/4 teaspoon salt
pepper to taste
4 tablespoons butter
2 tablespoons oil
1/4 cup chopped green onions
2 tablespoons chopped parsley
1 cup sliced mushrooms
1 cup chicken broth
2 tablespoons brandy
1 cup plain yogurt
1/2 cup chopped walnuts

Heat half the butter and oil in frying pan and quickly sauté the mushrooms. Set aside.

Season the breasts with salt and pepper, then flour lightly. Heat remaining butter and oil in large frying pan and brown chicken about 5 minutes on each side. Add green onions, parsley, brandy and broth. Bring to a boil, cover and reduce heat. Cook over low heat until tender, about 25 minutes.

Remove chicken from pan and place on serving platter. Keep warm. In pan, mix in yogurt, reserved mushrooms and walnuts, adding more broth if sauce appears thick. Bring to boil, then pour over breasts and serve with rice pilaf.

# Chicken & Rice with Sauce Cefalonia (Melaneza)

*This delicious combination only needs a salad, or vegetable dish of your choice for a wonderful feast.*

Place chicken in large pot with vegetables. Add enough water to cover generously and simmer at least one hour, or until tender. Remove chicken from stock. Clean from bones and cut into thin pieces, about 2 inches long. Cover and keep warm. Strain stock and taste; season lightly. Melt butter in skillet, lightly brown rice and add 5 cups of strained stock. Cover and cook over medium heat until rice is tender and stock is absorbed.

**Sauce:** Melt butter in saucepan, add flour and brown lightly, stirring constantly. Slowly add stock, milk, lemon juice and cheese and cook until thick and smooth. Spread half the rice on hot platter, pour half the sauce over rice, cover with the cut chicken meat, season with salt and cover with remaining rice and sauce. If desired, top with additional grated cheese.

1 chicken, about 3 pounds
1 small onion, quartered
2 stalks celery with leaves, cut in half
2 carrots, cut in half
4 tablespoons butter or margarine
2 cups converted rice, uncooked
salt and pepper to taste

**Sauce:**
1/2 cup butter or margarine
1 cup flour
1 cup milk
2 cups stock, or more
Juice of 1 1/2 lemons
1/2 cup grated cheese, Parmesan or Romano

# Chicken-stuffed Grape Leaves

*An alternative to the classic meat dolmas.*

3 cups ground turkey or chicken, raw
1 cup rice, raw
1/2 cup finely chopped green onions
1/2 cup finely chopped parsley
1/4 cup melted butter
1/2 teaspoon turmeric
1/8 teaspoon ground cloves
1 teaspoon salt, or to taste
1/4 teaspoon pepper
1 pound jar grapevine leaves

**Sauce:**
2 cups chicken broth
1/2 cup lemon juice
1 tablespoon tomato paste

Combine all ingredients except grapevine leaves, mix well. Wash grape leaves and drain. Place leaf, smooth side down, on large plate or board. Place about one heaping teaspoon filling at stem end and roll, tucking in the ends to enclose all the filling. Put a layer of torn or tough leaves to line the bottom of a heavy saucepan. Arrange rolls in layers.

**Sauce:** Combine above ingredients and pour over the grape leaf rolls. Put a heavy plate over the rolls, cover the saucepan and simmer for about 45 to 60 minutes. Cool, chill and serve with yogurt.

# Buffet Spinach-stuffed Chicken Breasts

*A Santa Barbara creation—made Greek-style with the addition of tangy feta.*

Sauté the onions in oil until soft. Combine with the other ingredients (except chicken) and mix well. Season highly.

Place each breast skin side up on a board. Trim away excess fat. Loosen skin from 1 side of breast and stuff approximately ⅓ cup of the filling under the skin. Tuck the skin and meat under the breast, forming an even, round, dome shape. Put the stuffed breasts in a buttered Pyrex or metal baking dish. Fifteen minutes before baking preheat oven to 350 degrees. Bake breasts until golden brown, about 30 to 35 minutes. Don't overcook or chicken will be dry. Cool slightly before serving, and cool at room temperature if you are going to slice into smaller serving pieces. Arrange on platters and decorate with fresh oregano and dill or other available herbs.

This is also a great choice for a small dinner party. Reduce the quantities above accordingly and serve by slicing the breasts crosswise and fanned on a plate to display the lovely spinach stuffing and placed in a pool of Béchamel sauce.

**Sauce:** Melt butter, stir in flour and salt. Add broth and wine and cook stirring constantly until mixture is thick and bubbly. Combine egg yolks with lemon juice. Stir half the hot mixture into egg, return to saucepan and cook for 2 more minutes, stirring constantly. Makes 3 cups sauce. Serves 24 as part of a buffet.

2 bunches green onion sliced thin
2 tablespoons olive oil
2 10-ounce packages frozen spinach
1 pound whole milk ricotta cheese
1 pound feta, crumbled
3 eggs slightly beaten
1/2 cup coarsely chopped Italian parsley
2 tablespoons fresh dill
Salt and freshly ground pepper taste
16 halves of chicken breast (order the chicken boned, split, with the skin on)

**Béchamel Sauce**
1/4 cup flour
3 cups chicken broth
1/4 cup butter
1/2 cup white wine
1/2 teaspoon salt
4 egg yolks
3 tablespoons lemon juice

# Skillet Chicken Greek-style

*An easy, very tasty chicken dish. Serve with a rice pilaf and village salad.*

1 cut-up fryer chicken, washed and dried
1 teaspoon salt
1/4 teaspoon pepper
1 teaspoon oregano
1/2 teaspoon paprika
1/4 teaspoon garlic powder
1/8 teaspoon turmeric, if desired
1/8 teaspoon sugar
1/2 cup lemon juice
olive oil
butter

Combine seasonings and season chicken pieces well. Place in bowl, pour the lemon juice over, and marinate for at least 1 hour or overnight. Drain chicken, flour the pieces and brown in hot oil and butter. Transfer browned chicken pieces to baking pan. Pour the lemon juice marinade into frying pan drippings, adding additional oregano, if desired. Stir juices together, pour over the chicken pieces in pan and cover with lid or foil. Bake at 325 degrees about 1¼ hours. Remove cover and continue baking additional 15 minutes until fork tender.

# Roast Chicken with Okra (Kota Me Bamyes)

*This is a favorite combination for okra enthusiasts.*

Wash and trim okra, leaving whole. Place in a bowl and marinate in one cup vinegar, 2 cups water and 1 tablespoon salt. Cover and allow to stand for one hour. Wash well and strain before frying in olive oil until lightly browned. Set aside. Cut chicken in serving pieces and brown in butter, set aside. In same pan, brown the chopped onion. Place the chicken pieces, okra and onions in casserole and add tomatoes. Season to taste. Bake at 375 degrees or until chicken and okra are tender. If casserole appears dry, add a little liquid (broth, white wine, or water).

1 4- to 5-pound chicken
1 medium onion, chopped
1 cup tomatoes, fresh or canned
1 1/2 pounds okra
1/2 cup butter
salt and pepper
marinade for okra

# Karpathian Turkey Stuffing (Paspara)

*A sweet and spicy alternative to other poultry dressings. It also makes a delicious side dish—try it topped with plain yogurt.*

1 pound ground beef
1 large onion, chopped
1 stick butter
1/2 cup pine nuts
1/2 cup rice (uncooked)
1/2 cup raisins (soaked in hot water and drained)
3 tablespoons tomato paste diluted with 3 tablespoons water
1/2 teaspoon each cinnamon and nutmeg
salt and pepper to taste
1 1/2 cups chicken stock

Sauté onions in butter until soft, add meat and brown well. Add spices, raisins, nuts and rice, transfer to casserole; add diluted tomato paste and blend well. Pour half the chicken broth over the mixture and bake at 350 degrees. In about 15 minutes, check to see if mixture seems dry. If needed, add remaining chicken broth and continue baking until rice is done.

# MEATS

# Meat and Macaroni Casserole (Pastitsio)

*One of the most famous Greek baked macaroni dishes. This is the Greek answer to lasagna—a great make-ahead dish.*

Brown meat with salt, pepper and 4 tablespoons butter. Add onion and parsley, brown well. Add tomato sauce and wine and simmer until liquid is absorbed, about 15 minutes.

Cook macaroni in boiling water with 3 tablespoons salt about 10 minutes. Do not overcook. Rinse and drain well. Combine macaroni with ½ cup melted butter and beaten eggs.

Butter an 11×14-inch pan, sprinkle with 2 tablespoons bread crumbs. Arrange half macaroni in pan, sprinkle with half the grated cheese and cover with meat mixture; spreading evenly over entire surface. Cover with remaining macaroni and grated cheese. Prepare cream sauce.

**Cream Sauce:** Melt butter, add flour and stir until slightly brown. Gradually add milk, stirring constantly until thickened. Slowly add beaten eggs and cook over very low heat until thickened. Season with salt and white pepper to taste. Spread cream sauce evenly over macaroni. Sprinkle with additional grated cheese. Bake at 350 degrees for 30 to 40 minutes until lightly browned on top. Serve warm.

**Note:** May be prepared ahead and cooked, then frozen. Defrost completely and reheat gently to serve.

2 pounds lean ground beef
2 teaspoons salt
1/4 teaspoon pepper
1 onion, chopped fine
2 tablespoons chopped parsley
3/4 cup butter
1 cup tomato sauce
1/2 cup red wine
1 pound macaroni (mostaccioli or ziti)
4 eggs, beaten
2 cups grated cheese (Romano or Parmesan)

**Cream Sauce:**
1/2 cup butter
8 tablespoons flour
4 cups warm milk
2 to 3 eggs

# Moussaka

*This most famous eggplant dish traveled from the Middle East and has become a Greek classic. We have lightened it somewhat for today's table.*

**Meat Mixture:**
1 1/2 pounds lean ground beef
1/2 cup butter
2 medium onions, chopped fine
1/2 can tomato paste
small glass red wine
salt and pepper to taste
2 tablespoons chopped parsley
2 eggs, well beaten
1/2 cup bread crumbs
2 medium eggplants
olive oil
grated cheese (Parmesan or
   Romano)

**Cream Sauce:**
1/4 cup butter
2 cups warm milk
2 tablespoons flour
1/2 cup grated cheese
3 eggs
salt and white pepper to taste
dash of nutmeg if desired.

Brown beef and onions in butter. Add parsley, tomato paste, wine, salt and pepper and cook until all liquid is absorbed. Add eggs and all but 1 tablespoon of the breadcrumbs. Mix well. Prepare eggplant: Peel and slice lengthwise. Soak in salted water 30 minutes; drain well. Brush hot griddle with oil and brown eggplant on each side, or broil eggplant slices brushed with oil until browned and softened. Butter a 9×13-inch pan and sprinkle with remaining breadcrumbs. Place a layer of eggplant. Top with cream sauce and sprinkle with remaining breadcrumbs. Place a layer of eggplant and sprinkle with a little grated cheese. Cover with meat mixture then add another layer of eggplant. Top with cream sauce and sprinkle with grated cheese. Bake at 375 degrees for 40 minutes or until nicely browned. Allow to set about 30 minutes before serving.

**Cream Sauce:** Melt butter in saucepan; add flour and stir until bubbly. Add warmed milk and cook until smooth and thickened. In blender or food processor beat the eggs with the grated cheese. Blend until smooth and add to milk mixture. Season with salt and pepper and cook until thickened. Add nutmeg. Pour over eggplant and sprinkle with additional grated cheese.

# Artichoke Moussaka

*For the artichoke lover, here is a delightful change from the classic moussaka.*

Brown meat and drain off fat. Lightly brown onions in butter; add browned meat and remaining ingredients. Cook 5 minutes, set aside.

**Cream Sauce:** Melt butter in 3-quart sauce pan; add flour and stir until bubbly. Add milk slowly, stirring constantly and simmer until thickened. Season with salt. Stir ¼ cup sauce into meat mixture. Beat eggs with cottage cheese and nutmeg, add to remaining sauce and cook 2 minutes more or until thick.

Butter a 9×13-inch baking dish. Sprinkle with bread crumbs. Arrange half the artichokes in baking dish, cover with half the meat mixture, sprinkle with half the grated cheese. Spoon half the sauce over the cheese. Repeat for second layer using remaining ingredients, ending with sauce. Dust lightly with additional grated cheese. Bake at 350 degrees for 1 hour, or until golden brown. Allow to set 10 to 15 minutes and cut into serving squares. Serves 10 to 12.

**Note:** May be prepared one day ahead and refrigerated. Reheat gently before serving.

**Meat Mixture:**
1/4 cup butter
2 large onions, finely chopped
2 pounds lean ground beef
2 cloves garlic, finely minced
1/2 cup dry red wine
4 tablespoons tomato paste
4 tablespoons chopped parsley
1/2 teaspoon cinnamon
salt and pepper

**Cream Sauce:**
1/4 cup butter
1/4 cup flour
3 cups lukewarm milk
1 teaspoon salt
3 eggs
2 cups small curd cottage cheese
dash nutmeg
1/2 cup bread crumbs
24 artichoke bottoms, canned
    drained, or 4 cans artichoke
    hearts, well-drained
1 1/4 cups grated cheese,
    Parmesan or kasseri

# Grape Leaves Stuffed with Meat (Dolmathes)

*We are all familiar with the grape-leaves-stuffed-with-rice mixture served as an hors d'oeuvre. Wrap the chopped meat filling with grape leaves; top with an egg-lemon sauce. A lot of work to prepare, but worth it!*

50 grapevine leaves, fresh or
   canned
1 1/2 pounds lean ground beef or
   lamb
1 large onion, finely chopped
1/4 cup parsley, chopped
1/4 cup mint leaves, chopped
   (optional)
1 1/2 teaspoons salt
1/4 teaspoon pepper
2 tablespoons olive oil
1/4 cup melted butter
1/2 cup tomato sauce
3/4 cup raw rice
water

**Avgolemono Sauce:**
3 eggs
juice of 1 lemon
1 cup broth from dolmathes
1 tablespoon cornstarch

Combine all ingredients except grapevine leaves and water, mix well. If using fresh leaves, wash thoroughly and blanch for half a minute. Canned leaves should be rinsed in hot water to remove brine. Place leaf, smooth side down, on a plate or board: Place 1 heaping teaspoon meat mixture in center of leaf. Starting at stem end, roll and enclose filling carefully. Have a large saucepan lined with coarse grape leaves and a few celery leaves. Arrange the filled leaves in compact layers. Place a heavy dish over rolls to prevent their breaking during cooking. Add one cup warm water, cover and simmer for 20 minutes. Add an additional cup warm water and cook another 20 minutes. When cool, drain off liquid for use in avgolemono sauce. You should have 1 cup liquid. If needed, add chicken broth to make 1 cup.

**Prepare Avgolemono Sauce:** Beat eggs well. Continue beating and slowly add the lemon juice. Dissolve cornstarch in 1 tablespoon water and add to egg mixture. Gradually add broth and blend well. Return broth to saucepan and cook over low heat until thickened, stirring constantly.

Immediately pour sauce over dolmathes and allow to set a few minutes before serving.

# Greek-style Meatballs (Keftedes)

*Make them small to serve as quick-disappearing appetizers or snacks—larger for lunch or dinner. Legendary in Santa Barbara.*

Mix all ingredients except flour and oil, until well blended. Form into balls, roll in flour and deep fry until golden brown and cooked through.

**Note:** If desired, substitute ½ pound ground turkey meat with half the ground chuck.

1 pound ground chuck
1 medium onion, chopped fine
1 clove garlic, chopped
2 teaspoons dried mint leaves, crushed
1/2 teaspoon oregano
1/2 cup chopped parsley (or 3 tablespoons dried parsley)
1/2 teaspoon salt
1/4 teaspoon pepper
1 egg
1/2 cup dried bread crumbs
flour
oil for frying

# Baked Meatballs (Keftedes)

*A hearty, but low-fat variation.*

2 pounds lean ground beef
1 large onion, grated
4 tablespoons finely chopped parsley
2 slices bread soaked in small amount of milk (remove crusts)
1 clove garlic, minced
1/2 cup white wine
2 eggs, beaten
1/2 teaspoon cinnamon
salt and pepper to taste
1/2 cup grated Parmesan cheese (optional)
1/2 cup melted butter

Mix together all ingredients except sauce and butter, until thoroughly blended. If mixture is dry, add small amount of water. Allow to stand for an hour or more, if possible. Shape into small balls. Place in pan with ½ cup melted butter. Bake at 400 degrees for 30 minutes. Add sauce, reduce heat to 350 degrees and continue to bake until done.

**Sauce:** Purée tomatoes in blender. Put in saucepan and add 1 cinnamon sugar. Cook over low heat for 15 minutes. Add to meatballs.

**Sauce:**
1 large can tomatoes
1 stick or dash of powdered cinnamon
1 tablespoon sugar

# Sausage-shaped Greek Meatballs (Soudzoukakia)

*A regional specialty of Smyrna, this ground meat mixture is spicy and satisfying—and not really a meatball at all.*

1/2 cup water
2 slices bread
2 cloves garlic, minced
2 teaspoon salt
1/2 teaspoon pepper
1 teaspoon ground cumin
1 egg, slightly beaten
1 1/4 pound ground beef
1/2 cup olive oil for frying

**Sauce:**
15-ounce can tomatoes
2 tablespoon olive oil
1/4 cup parsley

Pour water over bread slices, soak for 10 minutes, then mash with a fork. Add garlic, 1 teaspoon salt, ¼ teaspoon pepper, cumin, egg, and ground beef. Mix ingredients altogether and shape into 18 to 20 meatballs. Fry in olive oil until brown all over.

While you are frying the meatballs, prepare a tomato sauce with the tomatoes, olive oil, parsley, remaining salt, and pepper. Simmer for about 25 minutes. Add meatballs and cook over a low heat, uncovered, for 15 minutes longer. Serve hot with spaghetti or rice.

# Meatballs Avgolemono (Youvarlakia)

*Nothing is more delicious on a cold winter's night than a bowl of youvarlakia!*

Combine first six ingredients and knead to blend well; shape into balls. Bring chicken broth to boil and add meatballs. Add more broth if needed to cover the meatballs. Place lid on pan and simmer about 1 hour. Remove from heat and prepare sauce.

Beat eggs until frothy. Slowly add lemon juice and beat until thick. Add broth from Youvarlakia slowly to eggs and mix well. Pour sauce over meatballs and serve hot.

**Note:** Youvarlakia may be simmered in a mixture of water, ¼ cup tomato sauce and ½ cup butter instead of chicken broth.

2 pounds lean ground beef or ground turkey
1 onion, chopped fine
2 tablespoons chopped parsley
1/2 cup rice
1 teaspoon salt
1/4 teaspoon pepper
4 cups chicken broth (or more)
3 eggs
juice of 2 lemons (1/3 cup)

# Tomatoes Stuffed with Meat (Domates Yemistes)

*At the height of the tomato-growing season these stuffed vegetables not only look colorfully beautiful, but delicious too.*

12 large tomatoes
1 pound lean ground beef
2 tablespoons olive oil
1 large onion, finely chopped
1 small clove garlic, minced
3/4 cup long grain rice
1/4 cup chopped parsley
1 teaspoon oregano
1/2 teaspoon basil
1 teaspoon salt
1/4 teaspoon pepper
2 tablespoons tomato paste
1/4 cup white wine
1 cup hot water
1/4 cup pine nuts (optional)

Slice tops from tomatoes and set aside. Carefully scoop out pulp from tomatoes; chop and reserve pulp. Place tomato shells close together in oiled baking pan. Saute beef in oil until brown, add onion and garlic and cook 5 minutes. Add remaining ingredients and reserved pulp and cook 15 minutes, until rice is partially done. Fill tomato shells and replace tops. Pour an additional 1 cup hot water into pan and bake at 375 degrees for 30 minutes, basting occasionally with pan juices.

**Note:** Green peppers may be stuffed by following the method above and substituting one cup tomato juice for the tomato pulp.

# Beef Stew with Onions (Stifatho)

*Traditionally made in the villages with rabbit, but in the city it is much easier to find lean beef —or any stew meat used in equal amounts with onions. Cook it today and serve it tomorrow since it improves in flavor.*

Heat oil in skillet. Brown meat about 10 minutes. Transfer to larger cooking utensil, add onions. Combine remaining ingredients. Stir well and pour over meat. Place bag of spices in center of stew. Cover and bring to boil. Reduce heat to simmer and cook about 2 hours, or until meat is tender when tested. During cooking, add only enough water to keep liquid a thick consistency. This gravy may be thickened with a small amount of flour and water.

2 pounds lean stew meat
1 tablespoon olive oil
1 tablespoon butter
2 tablespoons red wine
4 cloves unpeeled garlic
2 tablespoons vinegar
6 tablespoons tomato paste
2 teaspoons salt
1/2 teaspoon pepper
2 cups hot water
2 tablespoons pickling spice (tied in a bag)
2 pounds small boiling onioins

# FACTS ABOUT LAMB

• Because of lamb's reputation for purity, the meat is not excluded from the diet of any religious sect or nationality.

• Early spring lamb is known as "Easter Lamb" and is used chiefly in connection with the religious ceremonies of the Greek population.

• Traditional barbecued lamb is cooked out of doors on a spit. According to legend, to see a lamb first when looking out of a window on Easter morning is considered a good omen, especially if its head is turned toward the house.

• Cooking instructions: Buy an entire lamb, have it cleaned. Wash and dry the lamb. Sprinkle with salt and pepper inside and out and fasten securely to a strong spit that is at least a foot longer on each end than the lamb. Secure at both ends and also at the center of the backbone to control turning of the lamb.

• Prepare the fire. The coals must be banked so that the maximum heat is aimed toward the thighs and shoulders and the least toward the breast. Rub the entire lamb with a marinade of one cup oil, juice of two to three lemons, a tablespoon each of oregano, salt, and pepper. Prepare more marinade if needed to use to baste periodically.

• A small lamb, 22 to 25 pounds, may be roasted in three hours. Larger lambs may need five to seven hours of slow cooking, plus frequent turning and basting.

• Lamb should be served hot or cold, never lukewarm.

# Roast Leg of Lamb

*Lamb is the traditional choice for festive dining, especially at Easter.*

Wash the meat well and place in roasting pan. In a small bowl mix salt and pepper with garlic. Make several incisions in the leg of lamb with a sharp knife and place slivers of garlic with the salt-pepper mixture into the cuts along with a little butter. Rub the outside of the lamb with the lemon, remaining butter (melted) and the remaining seasonings, including the oregano. Cover the roasting pan and cook at 325 degrees. Cook slowly. After the first hour, add wine to the liquid rendered in the pan and baste often with this until the meat is browned and done to taste.

In the last hour of cooking, small potatoes may be added around the lamb. When done, degrease and serve pan drippings with the roast.

**Note:** When the lamb is done, remove to platter to keep warm. Degrease pan drippings, add 3 cups hot water to drippings in pan and bring to boil on top of stove. Add 1 cup pasta (rosamarina or orzo), cover pan and place in hot oven (400 degrees) or on top of stove, for additional 20 to 25 minutes until pasta tests done. Adjust seasoning and serve sprinkled with grated Parmesan if desired.

5 to 6 pound leg of lamb
2 tablespoons butter
1 lemon
4 to 5 cloves garlic, peeled and
  slivered
1 cup white wine
2 tablespoons oregano
salt and pepper

**M
E
A
T
S**

# Lamb with Okra Casserole

*Traditional favorites, okra and lamb, combine in a tasty, savory dish.*

2 pounds boneless lamb cut in
   cubes
1/2 cup olive oil
1 onion, chopped
1/2 teaspoon cumin
1 cup peeled tomatoes
2 tablespoons tomato paste
1/2 cup stock or water
salt and pepper to taste
1 pound fresh okra
vinegar to cover
1 tablespoon butter or margarine

**Garlic Sauce:**
3 to 4 cloves garlic
1/4 teaspoon salt
2 tablespoons butter or margarine
I teaspoon ground coriander
Pinch of hot chili pepper (optional)

Brown meat in half the olive oil in a deep frying pan, transfer to a large casserole. Brown onion in meat drippings until soft. Add tomatoes, paste, stock or water with seasonings to onion mixture. Combine well and pour over lamb. Cover lab and cook over low heat until almost tender.

Place okra in a large bowl and add vinegar. Toss gently and let stand for 30 minutes. Drain and rinse well, then dry.

Melt 1 tablespoon butter, add okra and fry over medium heat for 3 minutes, stirring gently. Arrange okra on top of meat, cover and cook and additional 40 minutes, or until tender.

**Garlic Sauce:** Crush garlic with salt and place in skillet with 2 tablespoons butter until garlic is soft. Remove pan from heat, stir in coriander and chili pepper (if used) and add to lamb mixture. Heat through and serve over a bed of rice.

# Lamb with Artichoke Hearts Avgolemono

*Try the lamb with avgolemono sauce and artichoke hearts. Delicious!*

In a large skillet heat oil and saute onion until brown. Add meat and brown well on both sides. Add the wine, cover and simmer for 25 minutes. Add the water salt and pepper and simmer for one hour. In the meantime pour ¼ cup lemon juice over artichoke hearts and let set for approximately 15 minutes. Add artichoke hearts into meat and continue cooking until vegetables and meat is tender.

**Avgolemeno Sauce:** Beat egg whites until stiff. Add yolks one at a time beating after each. Add into eggs the hot stock from meat one tablespoon at a time (be careful that eggs don't curdle) or until eggs are warm alternating with ½ cup of lemon juice. Pour sauce over meat. Shake casserole well until sauce is blended into the meat and vegetables. Do not reheat meat because sauce will curdle. Serve warm.

3 pounds lamb shoulder or leg cut
   into 2-inch cubes
3 tablespoons olive oil
I large onion chopped
1/2 cup dry white wine
4 cups water
salt and pepper to taste
2 8-ounce frozen packages
   artichoke hearts

**Avgolemono Sauce:**
5 eggs separated
1/2 cup lemon juice
1 1/2 cups to 2 cups stock

# Lamb or Veal Casserole (Giouvetsi Me Kritharaki)

*Lamb, the king of Greek meats, is cooked in a variety of ways. This favorite is a one-dish meal.*

1 3-pound leg of lamb or veal rump roast
salt and pepper
garlic salt
1 small onion, chopped
1/2 cup dry red wine
2 cups water
1 1/2 cups canned tomatoes
4 cups boiling water
1 tablespoon salt
1 1/2 cups small rosamarina (pasta)
1/2 cup grated cheese (kefalotiri, Parmesan, or Romano)

Season meat with salt, pepper and garlic salt. Place in roasing pan and add chopped onion, wine and 2 cups water. Cover and bake at 325 degrees for two hours. Remove cover, raise heat to 400 degrees and bake 30 minutes longer, basting often. Remove meat to platter and cover to keep warm. Skim fat from pan juices. To remaining stock, add tomatoes, boiling water and salt. Return to 400-degree oven and let liquid come to a boil. Add the rosamarina and cook uncovered in oven for 20 minutes. All liquid should be absorbed. To serve, carve meat, arrange on platter and surround with the pasta. Sprinkle with grated cheese. Serves 6.

**Note:** Spaghetti or noodles may be substituted for the rosamarina

# Broiled Lamb Chops

*If you have the time to marinate the chops, the flavors are even more intense. Otherwise, brush the chops while broiling.*

Broil lamb chops. Blend all ingredients and spoon over broiled chops. Serve at once.

4 lamb chops
2 tablespoons lemon juice
1 teaspoon oregano leaves
1/4 teaspoon garlic powder
1 tablespoon olive oil.

# Lamb with Atzem Pilaf

*A good way to prepare the less expensive cut of lamb.*

Season meat with salt and pepper. Melt 1 tablespoon butter in large heavy saucepan. Add meat and onion and brown well. Add wine; cover and simmer 10 minutes. Add 2 cups boiling water, tomatoes and tomato sauce. Cover and simmer for about 2 hours, or until tender. Skim off fat. Add remaining 2 cups boiling water. Bring to boil again and add rice. Cover and cook 20 minutes. Melt the remaining two tablespoons butter and pour over the lamb and rice. Serve hot.

3 pounds shoulder lamb cut into serving pieces
3 tablespoons butter
2 onions, chopped
1/2 cup dry wine
4 cups boiling water
1 cup canned tomatoes
1/2 cup tomato sauce
1 cup rice
salt and pepper

# Braised Lamb with Greens (Arni me Horta)

*Spring in Santa Barbara gives a bounty of greens. Cook them with lamb for a fresh delicious stew.*

3 pounds lamb shoulder or necks
1 large onion, chopped
2 cloves garlic, minced
2 celery ribs, chopped
1 tablespoon olive oil
15-ounce can tomato sauce
1 cup white wine
salt and pepper
dash cinnamon
2 bunches greens, spinach, Swiss chard, endive or mustard greens
2 pounds French-cut green beans

Sauté onion, garlic and celery in olive oil until soft. Cut lamb into 1-inch cubes; add to vegetables and brown well. Season with salt, pepper and dash of cinnamon. Add tomato sauce and wine; cover and simmer until meat is almost tender. Carefully wash greens and cut to about 2-inches, add to lamb. Cook until greens are tender. Serve hot.

# Souvlakia

*The ever-popular meat on a skewer. You can substitute lean pork or beef if you wish.*

3 pounds lamb, beef, or lean pork, cubed
1/2 cup oil
1/3 cup lemon juice
1 teaspoon oregano
1 teaspoon garlic powder
salt and pepper
quartered onions, green pepper tomatoes and mushrooms, halved (mushrooms are optional)

Mix together oil, lemon juice, oregano, garlic powder, salt and pepper. Cut meat, onions, peppers and mushrooms in pieces and marinate for several hours or overnight. Skewer meat, alternating with vegetables, including tomatoes. Cook over charcoal or in oven broiler until done. Baste often with marinade. Serve over pilaf.

# Greek Sausage (Loukanikon)

*The distinctive flavor of orange imparts an aromatic, traditionally Greek approach to sausage.*

Have butcher grind the pork for sausage. Combine all ingredients except casings. Scald casings, dry, and using a sausage funnel, fill casings with mixture. Tie into desired lengths and make about three small punctures in each sausage. Allow to hang in a warm place for two days to drain. Store in refrigerator or freeze. To serve, fry slowly until well browned.

5 pounds boneless pork shoulder
1 cup dry red wine
3/4 cup finely cut dried orange peel
3 teaspoons salt
2 teaspoons black pepper
casings

# Mock Loukanikon

*When the Greek sausage (loukanikon) is not available, you can get similar taste by cooking sweet Italian sausage, or Polish sausage (whichever you prefer) with citrus.*

Cut the sausage into bite-sized pieces and brown in a heavy skillet. Cover skillet and continue cooking with a generous amount of thinly sliced oranges and lemons, until sausage is well cooked. Serve with a mustard sauce if you wish.

**Mustard Sauce:** Combine mayonnaise with nonfat yogurt, Dijon mustard, horseradish and mustard powder. Mix thoroughly and chill.

sausages

**Mustard Sauce:**
1/2 cup mayonnaise
1/3 cup nonfat yogurt
2 tablespoons Dijon mustard
1 tablespoon horseradish
2 teaspoons dry mustard powed

**M E A T S**

# Pork with Celery (Hirino Me Selino Avgolemono)

*The other California white meat. To add some zip to this stewed pork dish, serve with an avgolemono sauce.*

2 to 3 bunches celery
3 pounds lean pork, cubed
2 onions, chopped
1 clove garlic minced
4 tablespoons flour
1/2 cup white wine
2 cups water or broth
salt and pepper to taste

Clean celery stalks and remove strings from outer stalks. Cut into 2-inch pieces diagonally. Set aside. Brown pork cubes in butter with onions and garlic in butter in a Dutch oven. Add water and wine to cover and salt and pepper to taste. Cover and simmer 1½ hours or until almost tender, adding more water or broth as needed. Add celery to meat and simmer until celery is crisp buttered. Be careful not to overcook. Dissolve flour in ¾ cup water and add to mixture the last five minutes of cooking to thicken slightly. Remove from heat. Prepare avgolemeno sauce (page 31). Slowly mix the sauce into the prepared food. Shake pan gently so sauce is spread evenly throughout dish. Let sit for 5 minutes.

To serve, place pork and celery in large deep platter. Pour sauce over top and sprinkle with parsley. Delicious with crusty bread and salad. May be served with rice or mashed potatoes.

**Note:** Canned or frozen artichokes can also be added to this dish with the celery if desired. Serves 8.

# VEGETABLES

# Mixed Vegetable Casserole

*A colorful and delicious combination of vegetables.*

Wash and peel potatoes. Cut into ¼-inch slices. Arrange in a layer of the bottom of a 9×12-inch ovenproof glass dish. Sprinkle with salt and pepper and ¼ cup of the olive oil. Cut eggplant, zucchini, peppers and onions into ½-inch thick slices. Cut tomatoes into wedges. Pit olives. Arrange vegetables in rows on top of potatoes, keeping in mind the final effects of the colors and flavors. Distribute olives on top, sprinkle with salt and freshly ground pepper and remaining olive oil. Cover with a double thickness of foil. Bake for a 30 minutes at 375 degrees. Remove foil, reduce heat to 300 degrees and continue baking for 2 hours or until all vegetables are cooked. If vegetables seem dry, brush with oil or cover with foil for a few minutes.

Serves 10.

8 to 10 potatoes (3 pounds)
salt and freshly ground black pepper
3/4 cup olive oil
1 large eggplant
3 to 4 small zucchini (1 1/2 pounds)
1 yellow pepper
1 red pepper
1 green pepper
2 red onions
4 medium tomatoes
24 Kalamata olives

# Baked Mixed Vegetables (Tourlou Tava)

*Surely the French discovered Tourlou and thereby evolved Ratatouille! The Greeks add more vegetables to this wonderfully tasty combination.*

2 boxes frozen string beans, cut
2 boxes frozen baby okra
1 to 3 zucchini, cut in pieces
1 large eggplant, cut in pieces
4 stalks celery, cut in pieces
2 large onions, cut in eiqhths
4 cloves garlic, sliced
1/2 cup chopped parsley
salt and pepper
2 pounds tomatoes, fresh or canned
2/3 cup olive oil

Arrange first five vegetables in a 10×14-inch baking pan, insert onions and garlic throughout. Sprinkle with the parsley and salt and pepper. Break up tomatoes and cover vegetables. Add ½ cup water then dribble oil over vegetables; cover with foil and bake at 450 degrees until it begins to simmer; reduce heat to 350 degrees and continue to bake until vegetables are almost tender. Remove foil, add a little more water if necessary, and bake uncovered until vegetables are tender and slightly browned. Serve warm or cold.

# Filo-Wrapped Broccoli-Cheese Roll

*An elegant way to serve this ever-popular vegetable. Holds up well on the buffet table.*

1/2 pound filo dough
1/4 cup dried bread crumbs
1/2 cup melted butter or margarine
1 10-ounce package frozen chopped broccoli, thawed and well-drained
1/4 cup all purpose flour
11/4 cups milk
1/2 teaspoon salt
1/8 teaspoon cayenne pepper
4 ounces cheese (Swiss or Monterey jack) shredded

In a 2-quart saucepan, melt 4 tablespoons butter over low heat, stir in flour, salt and pepper until blended. Gradually stir in milk and cook, stirring constantly, until thickened and smooth. Add cheese and broccoli and cook until cheese is melted, stirring constantly. Remove from heat.

On waxed paper, overlap a few sheets of filo dough to make a 12×20-inch rectangle, brushing each sheet of filo with remaining melted butter. Sprinkle with 1 tablespoon crumbs. Continue layering buttered filo, sprinkling every third layer with 1 tablespoon crumbs. Preheat oven to 350 degrees. Spread broccoli mixture to cover about half the long end of rectangle. Beginning at broccoli edge, roll in jelly-roll fashion. You should have a roll 12 inches long. Place on cookie sheet, seam side down, score top and bake 35 to 40 minutes, until golden. Slice diagonally to serve.

**Note:** This may be prepared in a pan instead of rolled. Layer 6 sheets of filo, buttering each one, in a 9×13-inch pan. Spread the creamed broccoli evenly over the filo. Top with 6 to 8 more sheets of buttered filo. Score the top layers into desired size, sprinkle lightly with water and bake at 350 degrees for 35 to 40 minutes, until golden. Allow to cool slightly, then cut into the squares to serve.

# Eggplant Cheese Rolls

*The eggplant is the queen of vegetables in all Near Eastern cooking from Greece to Persia. Its origin is lost in time: some say it originated in India, but most probably, it was carried to Greece by the Arabs when they introduced the eggplant in the Middle Ages.*

1 large, round eggplant
2 tablespoons butter
2 tablespoons flour
1 cup milk, scalded
1/2 cup crumbled feta cheese
1 tablespoon minced parsley
1 tablespoon Parmesan cheese
salt, white pepper, nutmeg to taste
1 egg yolk
1/2 cup oil for frying
beaten egg
dry bread crumbs

Peel eggplant and slice ¼-inch thick. Place in colander and sprinkle with salt. Let drain for at least 1 hour. In saucepan, melt the butter, stir in flour and cook over low heat stirring for 3 minutes. Remove pan from heat, add the scalded milk in a stream, stirring vigorously with whisk until mixture is thick and smooth. Stir in cheeses, parsley and seasonings. Let mixture cool and stir in egg yolk.

Pat eggplant slices dry with paper towels and sauté in hot oil, adding more oil if necessary, until they are soft and lightly browned on both sides. Transfer to paper towels to drain. Put 1 to 2 teaspoons mixture in center of eggplant slice. Carefully roll up slices and press ends together. Dip the rolls in beaten egg, roll in dry bread crumbs, and dip again in the egg. (Note different method of breading.) Fry the rolls in hot deep oil (360 degrees) for 3 minutes or until golden brown. Remove with a slotted spoon and drain on paper towels. Serve as first course. Serves 6.

# Ionian Eggplant Casserole

*The influence of the Venetians produced this combination of eggplant with cheese. Or did the Venetians take it from the Greeks? Either way, the recipe remains delicious!*

Slice eggplant ½-inch thick and brown in hot oil until tender. Sauté garlic in olive oil, add tomatoes, tomato sauce and seasonings and simmer 30 minutes. Spoon some of the sauce in bottom of casserole, place a layer of eggplant over sauce, sprinkle with cheese, crumbs and additional salt and pepper. Repeat until all eggplant has been used, ending with tomato sauce. Sprinkle with grated cheese, bake at 350 degrees for 45 minutes.

2 medium eggplants
olive oil for frying
1 clove garlic, chopped
2 tablespoons olive oil
2 cans stewed tomatoes
1 can tomato sauce (8 ounces)
salt and pepper
dried oregano
Parmesan cheese
bread crumbs

# Green Vegetable Pie (Hortopita)

*This recipe uses a combination of assorted greens—make it as varied as you like. Some Greeks contend that you cannot have a decent hortopita without at least 35 different greens! Edible flowers such as calendula, nasturtium, and geraniums make a nice twist to this old favorite.*

4 medium zucchini, grated
1/4 pound fresh bulk spinach, washed and finely chopped
2 tablespoons Italian parsley, finely chopped
2 tablespoons fresh dill, finely chopped
1 tablespoon fresh mint, finely chopped
4 cups assorted greens, washed and chopped (beet tips, dandelions, watercress etc. If many different greens aren't available, substitute 4 more cups assorted greens for the 4 zucchini.)
1/2 cup bread crumbs
2/3 cup Parmesan cheese
6 large eggs, well beaten
salt and pepper to taste
sesame seeds

Put the zucchini and chopped greens in a large mixing bowl, and toss so they are evenly distributed. Mix the bread crumbs, cheese and eggs together and season with salt and pepper to taste. Pour over the greens and stir until everything is well mixed.

Grease 9×13-inch baking pan with olive oil. Put the mixture into it, smoothing the top. Sprinkle with sesame seeds. Bake in a preheated 350-degree oven for about 35 minutes, until the pie is springy to the touch. Serve hot or cold.

# Vegetarian Pastitsio

*Don't deny yourself the pleasures of pastitsio if you are a vegetarian. Here is a wonderfully delicious meatless version.*

Sauté onions and celery in olive oil until limp. Add carrots, continue sautéing another 3 to 5 minutes until soft. Add peppers and zucchini, adding more olive oil if needed, and sauté till tender. Add parsley, wine, tomato sauce and simmer until liquid is absorbed.

Cook pasta in salted water for 10 minutes. Rinse and drain well. Combine pasta with melted butter, cheese and eggs. Add vegetables and mix well. Place in an oiled 11×14-inch pan. Cover with Cream Sauce (recipe follows)

Bake at 350 degrees for 30 to 40 minutes, until lightly browned on top. Serve warm.

Melt butter, add flour and stir until slightly brown. Gradually add milk, stirring constantly until thickened. To beaten eggs, add milk mixture a little at a time, then return to pan and cook over very low heat until thick. Season with salt and white pepper to taste.

2 onions, finely chopped
6 carrots, shredded
4 celery stalks, finely chopped
2 red peppers, chopped
4 zucchini, shredded
1 bunch parsley, finely chopped
2 tablespoons olive oil (more as needed for sautéing)
1 cup white wine
2 cans tomato sauce
1 pound pasta (penne or mostaccioli)
1/2 cup melted butter
3/4 cup grated cheese (kefalotiri or Romano)
4 eggs, beaten

**Cream Sauce:**
1/2 cup butter
8 tablespoons flour
4 cups warm milk
2 to 3 eggs

# Meatless Pastitsio

*Forget "macaroni and cheese." This is a great way to combine pasta with sauce for a hearty main dish.*

12 ounces mostaccioli
1/2 cup butter or margarine
3/4 cup grated cheese (Parmesan or Romano)
1 cup cottage cheese

**Crema:**
1/2 cup butter or margarine
1/3 cup flour
6 cups warm milk
6 eggs
3/4 cup grated cheese (Romano or Parmesan)
1/2 cup cottage cheese
3/4 teaspoon salt

Cook mostaccioli per package directions. Drain, rinse and mix with remaining ingredients. Prepare crema.

Melt butter with flour, cook until bubbly, stirring constantly. Add enough milk slowly; stir until thickened. Beat eggs with remaining ingredients. Add milk mixture to eggs to warm, then return all to pan and cook over low heat until thick; stirring constantly. Taste for seasoning. Mix half the crema with the mostaccioli mixture, place in buttered 9×13-inch pan. Pour remaining crema on top and sprinkle generously with grated cheese. Bake at 350 degrees 45 minutes, or until nicely browned.

# Orzo & Feta-stuffed Tomatoes

*A colorful buffet dish.*

Cut ¼ inch of top off tomatoes. Scoop out pulp. Sprinkle insides with salt. Turn over and let drain for 30 minutes. Pat tomatoes dry. Mix orzo, cheese, olives, pine nuts, onions, parsley, olive oil, rosemary and garlic. Add lemon juice to taste. Season with salt and pepper. Spoon mixture into tomatoes. Cover and chill until ready to serve. Can be prepared one day ahead.

24 medium tomatoes
salt
6 cups cooked orzo (3 cups uncooked)
12 ounces feta cheese crumbled
11/2 cups chopped Greek olives
11/2 cups toasted pine nuts
11/2 cups chopped green onion
3/4 cup chopped fresh parsley
3/4 cup olive oil
11/2 teaspoon dried rosemary, crumbled
3 cloves garlic, minced
fresh lemon juice
salt and pepper to taste

# Stuffed Vegetables with Rice (Yemistes)

*A wonderful luncheon dish. All it needs is crusty bread and a chilled wine.*

4 tomatoes
2 green peppers
2 Japanese eggplants medium-sized
1 1/4 cup converted rice
2 medium onions, chopped
3 cloves garlic, minced
1/4 cup parsley, chopped
1/4 cup fresh mint, chopped
1 cup olive oil
1/4 teaspoon each salt and pepper
1/4 cup Parmesan cheese, if desired (optional)

Slice tops from tomatoes and carefully scoop out centers and save in a bowl. Slice tops from green peppers. Scoop out the inside and toss away. Slice one end of eggplant and scoop the inside out with a teaspoon. Place in bowl with tomatoes pulp, or you may cut eggplant in center lengthwise and scoop out both sides.

Place vegetables on a baking dish large enough so they fit tight together. In the bowl with the pulps, add the grated onion, garlic, parsley, mint and half the oil and pour into a blender. Mix all ingredients on medium speed until well blended. Pour back into the bowl. Add rice, salt and pepper, mix well. Fill vegetables with filling almost to the top. Sprinkle with Parmesan cheese. Cover vegetables with their tops and drizzle with remaining olive oil. Pour one cup of water in bottom of baking pan and bake at 350 degrees for approximately 90 minutes, or until rice is cooked and vegetables are soft.

# Vegetarian Moussaka with Potatoes

*Take a classic, like moussaka, and adapt it to today's vegetarian diet.*

Cut the potatoes into circles and fry in olive oil. Place on several layers of paper towels and pat dry with additional paper towels to remove any excess oil.

Meanwhile, begin cooking the rice according to package directions. After 20 minutes, add the tomatoes with their juice, the onion, parsley, garlic, salt and pepper. Bring back to a boil and simmer, until all liquid has evaporated.

Cover the surface of a 10×14×2-inch oven-proof dish with a little oil or nonstick cooking spray so the potatoes do not stick. Cover the bottom of the dish with half the potatoes, followed by the rice mixture, and the rest of the potatoes.

Make the Béchamel sauce and pour over the top layer of potatoes. Bake at 350 degrees until the surface turns golden brown. Allow it to cool before cutting into portions. Serves 8 to 12.

3 pounds potatoes
olive oil for frying
1 1/4 cups short-grain brown or
    white rice
1 pound canned tomatoes, drained
    and chopped (save the juice)
1 large onion, chopped
1/4 to 1/2 cup chopped Italian (flat-
    leaf) parsley
3 cloves garlic, finely minced
salt and pepper
Béchamel Sauce (see page 25)

# Spinach Pie from Trikala, Thessalia (Plastó)

*A very regional dish originating in northern Greece, where cornmeal is a staple. This is a variation of spanakopita.*

2 bunches spinach, washed,
    drained well and chopped
1/2 pound feta cheese, crumbled
3/4 cup olive oil
1/2 teaspoon dill weed
2 beaten eggs
1 bunch chopped green onion

**Cornmeal mixture:**
2 cups yellow cornmeal
4 1/2 cups water
1/2 cup milk
1/2 cup melted butter
salt

Mix together all ingredients and prepare cornmeal mixture.

Bring to boil the water, milk, butter and salt. Remove from heat and stir in the cornmeal.

**Method I:** Add cornmeal to spinach mixture and stir together until well mixed. Pour into greased 9×13-inch baking pan. Smooth top and dot with additional butter and sprinkle lightly with milk. Bake at 400 degrees for 1 hour or until nicely browned.

**Method II:** In a well greased 10×16-inch pan, spread half the cornmeal mixture. (If cornmeal appears too thick to spread, thin with enough milk to handle easily.) Gently spread the spinach mixture over cornmeal and level firmly by hand. Spread remaining cornmeal to completely cover spinach smoothing the top with your hand. With a table knife, score into squares. Drizzle with a little milk and olive oil. Bake at 400 degrees for 1 hour.

Cut into serving pieces and serve warm.

**Note:** May be prepared in advance and frozen before baking. Thaw slightly and increase baking time an additional 15 minutes.

# Spinach Turnovers

*When filo is not always available, a delicious vegetable "sandwich" is made with a crust strong enough to hold the spinach mixture. Make plenty. So easy to eat, they do not last long.*

**Crust:**
2 1/2 cups flour
1 rounded teaspoon salt
1/3 cup sugar
1 egg
1/3 cup corn oil
1/2 cup plus 2 tablespoons water

**Filling:**
2 bunches fresh spinach
2 tablespoons raw rice
1/2 cup corn oil
1/2 teaspoon pepper
1 tablespoon salt
1 tablespoon dried or fresh mint
1 tablespoon chopped parsley
1 large onion, minced
1 beaten egg

Add oil to flour and rub between hands. Beat egg with sugar and salt and add to flour and mix. Add enough water to make a smooth dough. Knead about 1 minute.

Thoroughly clean spinach and cut into 1-inch pieces. Salt spinach and let stand for about ½ hour. Drain thoroughly and squeeze out excess moisture. Combine with remaining ingredients.

To assemble, roll dough into oval shape and divide into 18 equal pieces. Roll each piece into circle, place heaping spoonful filling in half the circle and fold into turnover. Seal edges. Place on greased baking sheet, bake at 375 degrees for 20 minutes, until brown.

# Spinach & Rice (Spanakorizo)

*A Greek national treasure! A great combination to accompany any dish, especially fish. Spanakorizo can be made without the tomato sauce, substituting 1 cup water. Frozen chopped spinach may be substituted for the fresh.*

1 pound fresh spinach
1/3 cup olive oil
1 onion, chopped
1 1/2 cups hot water
1 8-ounce can tomato sauce
2 teaspoons salt
1/4 teaspoon pepper
1/4 teaspoon dill weed
1/2 cup converted rice

Wash spinach and cut into 1-inch pieces. Sauté onion in olive oil until golden. Add water, tomato sauce and seasonings and bring to boil. Add spinach and rice; cover and cook over low heat for 25 to 30 minutes. Serve with lemon wedges. Yields 6 servings.

# Stewed Green Beans (Fasolakia Yahni)

*A favorite method of cooking vegetables.*

2 cups chopped tomatoes
2 celery ribs, chopped
1 large onion, chopped
1 clove garlic, minced
1/2 cup chopped parsley
1/2 cup each olive oil and water
salt and pepper
2 pounds fresh or frozen green
    beans (French or cut)

Combine all ingredients except beans. Bring to high simmer and cook until vegetables are tender. Add beans and cook an additional 15 minutes.

# Artichoke Pita (Anginaropita)

*A delicious combination that traveled to Greece from Alexandria, Egypt. This perfect buffet dish is quite rich, but one piece will not hurt. Do not miss out on this pita.*

Cook artichoke hearts according to package directions. If they are large, cut into quarters. Butter a 9×13-inch baking pan and line with six sheets of filo, brushing each sheet with melted butter. Place half the artichoke hearts over filo. Beat eggs well with the grated cheese and cottage cheese, season with salt to taste. Pour half the egg mixture over artichokes. Cover with half the sliced cheese. Layer with 3 or 4 sheets filo, brushing each with melted butter. Repeat with remaining artichokes, egg mixture and cheese. Cover with at least 10 sheets of filo, brushing each sheet with melted butter. Sprinkle top lightly with a little water. Cut through top layers into diamond shapes, bake at 350 degrees for 45 to 60 minutes, until nicely browned. Serve warm.

Yield: 30 pieces

This pita can be completely prepared, allowed to cool, wrapped securely and frozen. Defrost and reheat gently to serve.

3 packages frozen artichoke hearts
1 pound filo dough
10 large eggs
1 cup grated cheese (Romano or kasseri)
1 cup small curd cottage cheese
1 pound melted butter
3/4 pound Swiss or Jack cheese, thinly sliced

# Spinach Pie (Spanakopita)

*No Greek ever grew up without Spanakopita. A favorite of everyone, even if not a spinach lover. A must on any buffet.*

2 bunches fresh spinach (2 pounds)
2 bunches green onions, chopped
1/2 cup olive oil
1 pound feta cheese, crumbled
6 eggs, well beaten
1/2 cup chopped parsley
1/4 teaspoon dried dill weed
1/2 pound filo dough
1/2 pound melted butter
salt and pepper to taste

Clean and chop spinach, salt well, and place in colander to drain thoroughly. Squeeze out any excess moisture from spinach and place in large bowl. Sauté onions in olive oil until lim and add to spinach. Add cheese and seasonings, being careful not to oversalt. Add eggs and blend well. Butter a 9×13-inch pan and place 6 pastry sheets into pan, brushing each with melted butter. Spread spinach mixture evenly over filo and cover with 6 additional pastry sheets, brushing each with melted butter. Score top layers of filo into squares and bake at 350 degrees for approximately one hour or until golden brown. Cut the squares completely and serve hot or cold.

**Note:** If desired, substitute the 1 pound of feta with ½ pound feta and one cup cottage cheese.

# Zucchini Casserole (Kolokithia Yahni)

*A traditional, basic dish—especially wonderful when made with garden-grown zucchini and tomatoes.*

1 pound zucchini squash (cut 1-inch pieces)
1/2 cup olive oil
1/4 cup chopped onion
1/2 cup tomatoes
chopped parsley
1/4 cup water, if needed
salt and pepper to taste

Brown chopped onion in olive oil. Add tomatoes, chopped parsley, salt and pepper and bring to boil. Place cut zucchini in casserole and cover with sauce. Cover casserole and simmer until done. Sauce should be thick.

# Zucchini Pie (Kolokithopita)

*Dress up your zucchini with feta and filo dough—a tasty alternative to spanakopita.*

Grate zucchini, salt lightly and allow to drain. Sauté onion in the 1 tablespoon butter and oil. Stir in rice, ¾ cup water, cover and cook until water is absorbed. Add squash and cook an additional 5 minutes. Remove from heat and allow to cool. Beat eggs well, blend in cheese and add to squash mixture. Season to taste with salt and pepper.

Butter a 10×15-inch baking pan and line with six sheets of filo dough, brushing each sheet with melted butter. Add squash filling and cover with eight sheets filo, brushing each sheet with melted butter. With a sharp knife, score top filo sheets lightly into serving-size pieces. Bake at 350 degrees for 15 minutes, reduce heat to 325 degrees and bake an additional 30 minutes. Serve warm.

1/2 pound filo dough
1/2 pound butter, melted
3 pounds zucchini squash, grated
1 large onion, chopped
1/2 cup raw rice
10 eggs
1 tablespoon butter
1/4 cup olive oil
1/2 pound crumbled feta cheese

# Zucchini Fritters

*You can't have too many ways to prepare this prolific vegetable.*

1 cup shredded zucchini
1/4 cup shredded leeks
1/3 cup kefalotiri or Parmesan
  cheese, grated
1/2 cup bread crumbs
3 tablespoons Italian parsley, finely
  chopped
2 tablespoons fresh mint, finely
  chopped
2 large eggs
salt and pepper
olive oil for frying

Place the shredded zucchini in a colander, salting well, and let drain for 20 minutes. Rinse and squeeze out any excess liquid. Combine all the ingredients in a bowl, stirring until they are evenly distributed.

Put ½ inch of oil in a large pan. Heat until very hot (oil will sputter loudly when sprinkled with 1 to 2 drops water). Put heaping teaspoons of the mixture in the oil and fry until golden brown, turning once. Do not cook too many at once or the temperature of the oil will decrease, causing the fritters to absorb too much oil and become greasy. Drain on paper towels and serve hot.

# Fried Zucchini and Eggplant

*Tasty, simple, and really good!*

zucchini
eggplant
oil for frying
flour

Wash eggplant and slice crosswise in ½-inch slices. Sprinkle with salt and set aside. Wash zucchini and slice lengthwise in ⅛-inch slices. Salt and set aside. This will allow the vegetables to render some of their moisture.

Pour ¼ inch cooking oil, corn, canola or olive oil, in skillet. When oil is hot, roll several slices of the vegetable in flour and fry a few at a time until browned. Drain on paper towels and serve.

**Variation:** Sprinkle cooked vegetables with vinegar before serving, or sprinkle with garlic salt before frying.

# Fried Cauliflower with Lemon (Kounoupithi Tiganito)

*A tasty way to prepare often boring cauliflower.*

cauliflower
lemon juice
vegetable oil
flour

Separate cauliflower into flowerets. Cook in boiling water with the juice of half a lemon until tender, but not soft. Drain thoroughly. Dredge in flour and deep fry until golden brown. Season to taste. Sprinkle generously with lemon juice and serve hot

# Lima Bean Casserole (Gigantes)

*An excellent Lenten dish. This peasant dish has been a staple in the mountains of northern Greece and now it can be found in the tavernas of the Plaka. Serve these beans with peasant bread for a delicious meal, along with a village salad!*

Boil beans in large pot of water (about 8 cups) until tender, but not falling apart—about 45 minutes. Drain beans and save water.

Place beans in a 6-quart casserole dish. Add all remaining ingredients and mix together. Pour in enough of the saved water to just cover top of beans. Cover casserole dish and bake at 425 degrees for one hour.

Remove from oven. If beans are tender, check for seasoning, remove lid, sprinkle cheese on top if desired, and return to oven uncovered for 30 to 45 minutes adding enough water to keep beans moist. Check and remove when beans are brown and almost crunchy on the top and have formed a sauce. If they appear dry, just carefully add more water. Serves 6 to 8.

1 pound dried large lima beans rinsed
1 large can stewed, chopped tomatoes with juice (about 2 cups)
1 large onion, chopped
6 cloves garlic, chopped
1 teaspoon dried dill (use fresh if available)
3 tablespoons olive oil*
salt and pepper to taste
Parmesan cheese (optional)

*For a "no-added fat recipe," omit oil and Parmesan cheese. You will need more liquid to take the place of the oil.

# Baked Potatoes Riganates

*A wonderful way to prepare this basic vegetable.*

6 large potatoes or more
1 tablespoon dried oregano leaves
1 teaspoon salt
1/4 teaspoon pepper
1/2 cup lemon juice
1 cup vegetable oil
2 cups chicken broth, or 2 bouillon
    cubes dissolved in 2 cups
    water

Peel potatoes and cut into wedges. Put in a large baking pan to make one layer. Mix lemon, oil and seasonings and pour over the potatoes. Add broth to bottom of pan and bake at 350 degrees until potatoes are tender. Add a little hot water if potatoes seem dry.

**Note:** These potatoes take a while to cook, up to 2 hours, but are very delicious.

# Pasta with Browned Butter & Cheese (Macaronatha)

*This is absolutely delicious with fresh Parmesan and, if available, a dried ricotta. Simple to prepare—delicious when served.*

1 pound long macaroni
1/4 cup butter
grated cheese, Parmesan or
    Romano

Boil macaroni in salted water until tender. Drain well. Melt butter until light brown. Sprinkle cheese on large serving platter; lay half the macaroni over cheese. Sprinkle with grated cheese and drizzle with a little butter. Add the remaining macaroni and repeat with grated cheese and top with butter. Serve with village salad.

# Chicken-flavored Manestra

*A favorite pasta shaped like cantaloupe seeds. Serve alongside a main dish of chicken.*

Brown manestra in butter. In a separate pan, combine broth, tomato sauce, oregano and lemon juice; bring to boil. Add to manestra, cover and cook over low heat until broth is absorbed and manestra is tender. Stir often to avoid sticking. If it appears dry, add additional broth. Serves 6.

4 tablespoons butter
1 cup manestra (orzo or rosamarina)
3 1/2 cups chicken broth
1/2 cup tomato sauce
generous pinch oregano leaves
juice of 1/2 lemon

# Beef-flavored Manestra

*Wonderful with any meat entrée. Note the variation for lamb.*

Brown manestra in butter. Add beef stock, tomatoes and garlic powder. Cover and cook over low flame until manestra is tender. Stir often to avoid sticking. Add salt and pepper to taste. Serves 6.

Note: When preparing roast leg of lamb, use the pan drippings with the beef broth.

4 tablespoons butter
1 cup manestra
3 1/2 cups beef stock
1/2 cup canned tomatoes or tomato sauce
1/8 teaspoon garlic powder
salt and pepper to taste

# Rice Pilafi

*A classic. No Greek kitchen would be without a supply of long-grain white rice. The grains cook up fluffy and not sticky.*

1/4 cup butter
2 cups long grain white rice
4 cups chicken broth

Melt butter in heavy skillet and lightly brown rice, stirring constantly. This takes approximately 5 minutes. Bring chicken broth to a boil and add to rice. Cover and reduce heat. Simmer 20 minutes until liquid is absorbed and rice is tender. Do not stir. (Diced chicken may be added to rice if desired.)

To serve, butter inside of cup, spoon in rice and pack tightly. Unmold on heated plate and serve with Savory Tomato Sauce I (see recipe on page 30).

# DESSERTS

# Festival Baklava

*Of Byzantine origin, it is the aristocrat of pastry sweets. Found throughout the Near East.*

Prepare the syrup first. Bring to a boil (219°F on candy thermometer) the first four ingredients with slices of orange. Add lemon juice and boil again to 220 degrees. Allow to cool. Pour cooled syrup evenly over hot baklava.

Combine walnuts, spices, crumbs and sugar in a large bowl. Brush bottom of 12×18-inch pan with butter, place first filo sheet in pan. Brush with butter and layer with 5 more sheets filo, brushing each sheet with melted butter. Keep remaining filo covered with plastic wrap and slightly damp towel. Sprinkle buttered filo evenly with nut mixture. Cover with 4 sheets filo, brushing each with butter. Sprinkle nuts and continue in this manner until all nuts are used. Top with 10 sheets filo, buttering each sheet. Brush top generously with remaining butter. Before baking, cut pastry into diamond shapes, being careful not to cut through to the bottom layer. Sprinkle top very lightly with water. Bake at 300 degrees at least 1 ½ hours. Check to see that the middle layers of filo are crisply baked, not soft. Remove from oven and immediately pour cooled syrup over it, slowly. Let stand 24 hours. To serve, cut baklava through to remove from pan.

**Syrup:**
4 cups sugar
3 cups water
1/2 cup honey
1 stick cinnamon
2 tablespoons lemon juice
small orange, sliced

**Pastry:**
1 1/2 pound filo dough
1 1/2 pound sweet butter, melted
6 cups walnuts, medium grind
3 teaspoons cinnamon
1/8 teaspoon ground cloves
1/2 cup granulated sugar
1/2 cup graham cracker crumbs

# Baklava Rolls (Saragli)

*A version of baklava in jelly-roll fashion.*

4 cups chopped walnuts
2 teaspoons cinnamon
1/2 teaspoon nutmeg
1/2 cup sugar
1 pound filo dough
1 pound sweet butter

**Syrup:**
2 cups sugar
1 1/4 cups water
1 teaspoon lemon juice or sliced
   lemon

Combine walnuts, spices and sugar; set aside. Melt butter and clarify by allowing solids to remain in bottom of pan. Spread out one sheet filo dough, sprinkle with 3 tablespoons nut mixture. Lay a second sheet over nuts and repeat until you have three layers filo and nuts. Beginning with long edge, roll tightly, jelly-roll fashion. Cut into 1-inch pieces and set upright in baking pan. Cover with a damp tea towel while continuing with rest of filo and nut mixture until all ingredients are used. Bring clarified butter to boil. Spoon one tablespoon at a time over each roll, using all the butter. Bake at 350 degrees for about 30 minutes, until lightly brown. Remove from oven and spoon cooled syrup over each roll. Let cool completely for 3 hours, turn each roll over and set in platter to serve.

**Syrup:** Bring to a boil, simmer to 225 degrees on candy thermometer, to a fairly thick syrup. Let cool. For a different flavor, add 2 drops of oil of Bergamot.

# Shredded Filo Pastry (Kataifi)

*This kataifi pastry rivals baklava in popularity. The dough is more fragile than filo and therefore even more of a challenge to prepare.*

Open the kataifi pastry and carefully spread half evenly over the bottom of a 9×12-inch baking pan. Drizzle with half the melted butter. Combine the nuts, ½ cup sugar and cinnamon in a small bowl. Spread the nut mixture over the kataifi pastry dough and cover with the remaining dough. Brush or drizzle with the remaining butter and bake at 350 degrees for 40 minutes or more until golden. Remove from oven and spoon the hot syrup over pastry. Cover with a dry towel and allow to cool thoroughly. Cut into square or diamond shapes of desired size. Dust with additional ground cinnamon for serving if you wish.

**Syrup:** Boil the remaining 3 cups sugar with water for 5 minutes, stir in the honey and lemon juice, bring to boil and keep hot.

**Note:** Kataifi can also be prepared in individual rolls. Divide kataifi into lengthwise sections about 4 inches wide. On one end of each pastry section, place 2 teaspoonfuls of nut mixture. Roll up to end and place on a buttered baking sheet. Repeat until all pastry is rolled and lined up, not too tightly in the pan. Brush or spoon melted butter on each roll and bake for approximately 35 minutes, or until golden. Remove from oven and spoon the hot syrup over the pastry. You may need to double the amount of melted butter.

1 pound commercial kataifi pastry (available in specialty Greek markets)
1 1/2 cups melted unsalted butter
1 1/2 cups blanched finely chopped almonds or walnuts
3 1/2 cups granulated sugar
1 tablespoon cinnamon
2 cups water
1/2 cup honey
2 tablespoons lemon juice

# No-Bake Kataifi

*Reminiscent of the classic pastry, but a simplified version.*

2 large boxes Shredded Wheat
2 cups chopped walnuts, medium
    fine
1 pound melted butter
2 teaspoons cinnamon
1 tablespoon grated orange rind
syrup

**Syrup:**
6 cups sugar
4 cups water
juice of 1 orange and grated rind
juice of 1 lemon and grated rind

Crumble Shredded Wheat fine in a large bowl (removing any hard ends). Combine melted butter and syrup. Add syrup (reserving ¾ cup) to Shredded Wheat to moisten thoroughly. Pat half the mixture in buttered 9×13-inch pan. Combine nuts, spices and rind and sprinkle half over Shredded Wheat. Pat remaining wheat mixture and top with remaining nut mixture. Drizzle remaining syrup over all. Refrigerate. Cut into desired shape.

**Syrup:** Combine ingredients and boil for 20 minutes. May not be necessary to use all syrup on top of pastry.

# Almond Rolls (Froï Glacé)

*Ground almonds and glazed fruit rolled in filo dough for a delightful sweet.*

Melt butter and keep warm in a saucepan. Beat egg yolks until thick and light in color. In a separate bowl, combine almonds and sugar and mix until well blended. Add vanilla and mix well. Stir in egg yolks.

In a medium-size bowl, beat whites until stiff. Fold egg mixture into whites until all is well blended.

On a flat surface spread 6 to 8 sheets of filo and butter each layer. Place ¼ of the filling along the narrow edge of fillo in center. Sprinkle with chopped candied fruit ( do not mix fruit into the filling). Fold like a jelly roll. (Fold over once to cover filling, then once along outer edges to enclose filling. Roll tightly to end of filo). Place on buttered cookie sheet. Butter the top of roll. Repeat the same procedure with the remaining filling and filo to make 3 more rolls. Bake at 350 degrees approximately 30 minutes until golden brown. Remove from oven and let cool for 10 minutes. Cut into sections approximately 1½ inches thick and place each piece flat on a buttered cookie sheet. Bake again for approximately 5 minutes until light brown on top. Cool cakes.

**Syrup:** Boil all ingredients until syrup reaches 210 degrees on a candy thermometer. Pour hot syrup over cold rolls. Let cool completely before serving. Makes 4 rolls, 12 to 15 pieces per roll.

6 egg whites
5 cups ground almond
2 egg yolks
1 pound sweet butter
1 pound filo
3 pounds candied colored fruit, chopped
1 cup sugar
I teaspoon vanilla

**Syrup:**
3 cups sugar
2 cups water
2 cinnamon sticks
2 whole cloves
1/2 cup honey
3 tablespoons lemon juice

# Custard Pastry (Galatoboureko) I

*A rich custard pie made elegant with a crust of crisp filo. It is best served the same day or the following day. Keep in a cool area and cover with a tea towel to keep filo crispy. Any leftover pastry should be refrigerated.*

8 cups milk (2 quarts)
1 1/2 cups Cream of Wheat or Farina
1 1/2 cups sugar
12 eggs separated
1 pound unsalted butter
1 pound filo dough
1 teaspoon vanilla
1/4 cup grated orange peel
1/4 cup grated lemon peel
2 cinnamon sticks
2 whole cloves

**Syrup:**
1 1/2 cups water
3 cups sugar
1 tablespoons lemon juice
2 cinnamon sticks
2 whole cloves
2 slices each lemon and orange

Prepare syrup and cool: Bring all ingredients to boil, except lemon juice, for approximately 30 minutes. Add lemon juice and boil gently for additional 20 minutes. Let cool completely.

Cook milk, Cream of Wheat, sugar, orange and lemon peel, cinnamon sticks and cloves on medium heat stirring constantly until thickened. Remove from heat. Remove cinnamon sticks and cloves and discard. Separate eggs. Beat egg yolks until light. Beat egg whites to form stiff peaks. Fold egg yolks into whites, add to milk mixture very slowly mixing continuously until well blended. Add vanilla and mix well.

Butter an 11×17-inch baking pan. Place 6 to 8 sheets of filo dough on bottom of pan buttering every other sheet. Pour custard over filo evenly. Cover with remaining filo dough brushing each sheet with melted butter. Sprinkle top sheet with a little water and bake at 350 degrees for 45 minutes to one hour. Test with toothpick in center of filling. Toothpick should come out clean. Cut into square serving pieces. Spoon cooled syrup over top.

# Custard Pastry (Galatoboureko) II

*A simpler version of the popular custard pastry.*

6 cups milk
2 cups sugar
1 cup minus 2 tablespoons Cream
   of Wheat (uncooked)
1 pound unsalted butter
1 teaspoon vanilla
12 eggs, separated
1 pound filo dough

**Syrup:**
1 cup water
3 cups sugar
strips of rind from 1 lemon

Cook milk, vanilla, 1 cup sugar, 1 cup butter and Cream of Wheat until slightly thickened, stirring constantly. Remove from heat, set aside. Stir occasionally. Beat egg yolks with 1 cup sugar until thick, set aside. Beat egg whites to form stiff peaks; set aside.

While milk mixture is still warm, add yolk mixture and stir to blend thoroughly. Fold in egg whites.

Butter an 11×17-inch pan; place 7 layers of buttered filo dough, making sure edges of filo come to top edge of pan. Pour custard over filo, spread evenly. Cover with 7 layers of buttered filo. Fold edges to enclose filling.

With sharp knife, cut through top few layers of filo, into diamond shapes. Bake at 350 degrees for 45 to 60 minutes, until custard tests set with toothpick. Let cool.

**Syrup:** Combine ingredients and boil 15 minutes, remove rind and slowly spoon syrup over pastry. When pastry has completely cooled, cut through to serving pieces. Store in refrigerator.

# Potinga

*This is a light, nutty custard—delicious and simple to prepare.*

4 cups milk
1 cup sugar
1/2 cup butter
5 eggs
2 teaspoons vanilla
3/4 cup Cream of Wheat (not instant)
1 teaspoon cinnamon
1/2 cup pecans, chopped fine
whipped cream (optional)
candied cherries (optional)

**Syrup:**
1 cup sugar
1 cup water

Combine the milk, butter and sugar in a large saucepan. Heat to boiling. Gradually add Cream of Wheat, stirring continuously until bubbling. Remove from heat. Cool 15 minutes, stirring occasionally to prevent crusting. Add cinnamon and vanilla. Beat eggs well and slowly stir into mixture. Fold in chopped nuts. Pour into buttered 8×12-inch baking dish. Bake 35 minutes at 375 degrees. Remove from oven.

**Prepare syrup:** Bring sugar and water to a boil. Slowly spoon syrup evenly over the pastry. When completely cool, cut into diamond shapes. If desired, garnish with a dab of whipped cream and candied cherries. Refrigerate the remaining pastry.

# Festival Yogurt Cake

*Another Santa Barbara Greek Festival favorite—lovely when cut into diamond shapes and placed in paper cupcake cups.*

Prepare syrup. May be made a day or two ahead. Combine sugar, water and orange slices. Bring to a full boil and add lemon juice. On low heat, continue to simmer until slightly sticky, about 1 hour. Allow to cool.

Melt butter and let stand till cooled. Pour into mixing bowl and beat at high speed until light. Separate eggs. Beat egg yolks in a separate bowl. Add to butter and blend at low speed. Add sugar and continue blending until light, being careful not to over beat. Blend in yogurt. Combine cream of wheat, flour, baking soda, baking powder and grated rind in a large bowl and add to mixture, blending thoroughly. Beat reserved egg whites until stiff, fold into batter. Pour into greased 9×13-inch pan and bake at 325 degrees for 45 to 50 minutes, or until cake tests done in the center. Remove from oven and immediately cut into diamond or triangle shapes and pour 1½ cups *cold* syrup over *hot* cake. Let cake cool completely before serving. Place in foil baking cups to serve.

May be frozen. Allow to thaw to room temperature to serve.

3/4 pound sweet butter
8 eggs separated
2 cups sugar
2 cups plain yogurt
2 cups quick Cream of Wheat (not instant)
1 1/2 cups flour
2 teaspoons baking soda
1 teaspoon baking powder
1/4 cup orange rind

**Syrup:**
2 cups sugar
3 cups water
1 tablespoon lemon juice
1 orange, sliced

# Almond Yogurt Cake (Yaourtini)

*A moist yogurt cake laced with cognac and spices.*

1 cup butter
2 cups sugar
6 eggs
1 cup plain yogurt
2 teaspoons baking soda
2 ounces cognac
2 cups flour
1 teaspoon ground cloves
1 teaspoon cinnamon
1 cup almonds, finely chopped

**Syrup:**
2 cups sugar
3 cups water
1 tablespoon honey
juice of 1/2 lemon

Combine syrup ingredients and boil for 20 minutes. Cool.

Melt butter and allow to cool.

With electric mixer, beat butter and gradually add sugar, creaming well. Add eggs, one at a time, beating well after each addition. Stir in yogurt. Combine soda and cognac and add to mixture. Add the dry ingredients and blend well. Blend in the almonds.

Pour into a well-buttered 12x17-inch pan. Bake at 350 degrees 45 to 55 minutes, or until cake tests done when a toothpick inserted into the center comes out clean. Cool slightly and spoon cooled syrup slowly over cake. Cut into diamond shapes to serve.

# Orange-flavored Yogurt Cake

*Almonds, yogurt, and orange combine in a delicious treat.*

Combine syrup ingredients, bring to boil and simmer 20 minutes. Remove orange and allow to cool completely.

Meanwhile, in a large mixing bowl, cream butter and sugar until mixture is light and fluffy. Add egg yolks, one at a time, beating well after each addition. Add orange extract and rind to yogurt and stir into egg mixture. Sift flour with baking powder and soda and add alternately with milk, blending thoroughly. Stir in almonds, if used. Beat egg whites until stiff and fold into batter. Pour into well buttered 9×13-inch pan, bake at 350 degrees 50 to 60 minutes, or until cake springs back when touched and is medium brown on top. While still hot, spoon cooled syrup over cake. Let stand at least 6 hours or overnight before serving.

1 cup butter
1 1/2 cups sugar
5 eggs, separated
3 cups sifted cake flour
3 teaspoons baking powder
1/2 teaspoon baking soda
1/2 cup milk (or 1/4 cup milk with
   1/4 cup orange juice)
1 cup plain yogurt
1/2 teaspoon orange extract
1 teaspoon grated orange rind
1 cup almonds, finely ground
   (optional)

**Syrup:**
1 1/2 cups sugar
2 cups water
slice orange with rind, 1/2-inch
   thick

# Yogurt Cake (Yaourtopita)

*A healthy cake—flavored with orange, Cream of Wheat, and plain yogurt.*

3/4 pound butter or margarine
8 eggs, separated
2 cups sugar
2 cups plain yogurt
1 1/2 cups quick Cream of Wheat
   (not instant)
1 1/2 cups flour
2 teaspoons baking soda
1 teaspoon baking powder
grated rind of 1 orange or lemon

**Syrup:**
2 cups sugar
3 cups water
juice of 1 lemon

Melt butter and let stand until cooled and pour into large mixing bowl. Add egg yolks two at a time, blending well with wooden spoon. Add sugar and continue blending until light being careful not to overbeat. Blend in yogurt.

Combine Cream of Wheat, flour, baking soda, baking powder and grated rind in a separate bowl. Add to egg mixture, blending thoroughly. Beat egg whites until stiff and fold into batter. Pour into well buttered 12 x 16-inch pan. Bake at 350 degrees for 30 minutes, or until a toothpick into the center of the cake comes out clean. Cool cake, cut into diamond shapes and slowly spoon hot syrup over cake. Allow to stand 6 hours or overnight before serving.

Combine the sugar and water for syrup and boil gently for 25 minutes. Add lemon juice and boil an additional 5 minutes. While hot, spoon over cooled cake.

# Pantespani with Milk Cream & Lemon Pudding Fillings

*A very rich torte intended for special occasions.*

Bring all syrup ingredients to a full boil and let syrup simmer for approximately 45 minutes. Let syrup cool completely

Prepare Pantespani by beating yolks well. Add sugar and beat 5 minutes. Then add rest of the ingredients one at a time, beating after each addition. Beat whites in separate bowl until stiff. Fold yolk mixture into whites until well blended and pour into a 10×15-inch buttered pan. Bake at 350 degrees for 40 to 45 minutes. Pour cold syrup over hot cake and set aside to cool completely.

Mix some of Milk Cream ingredients (sugar, cornstarch, salt and 1 cup milk) in sauce pan and cook slowly until all ingredients dissolve. Stir constantly so it will not stick to the bottom of the pan. Then add the rest of the milk. Cook until thickened. Remove from heat, let set for 10 minutes then pour over Pantespani cake. Refrigerate for 2 hours.

Prepare Lemon Cream. Mix sugar, cornstarch and 1 cup of the water in sauce pan and cook slowly until all ingredients dissolve. Stir constantly so it will not stick to the bottom of the pan. Then add the remaining water, lemon juice, and vanilla, and cook until thickened. Remove from heat and let set for 10 minutes. Pour over milk cream. Refrigerate for 2 hours.

Beat whipping cream until stiff. Spread to cover cake. Decorate with strawberries or cherries or fresh mint leaves.

**Syrup:**
2 cups sugar
1 1/2 cups water
2 tablespoons lemon juice

**Pantespani:**
10 eggs separated
2 cups sugar
2 oranges squeezed and grated
2 cups semolina or farina
1/4 cup liqueur (Amaretto or other)

**Milk Cream:**
1/2 cup sugar
6 tablespoons cornstarch
1/4 teaspoon salt
4 cups milk
1 1 /2 teaspoon vanilla

**Lemon Cream:**
3/4 cups sugar
8 tablespoons cornstarch
5 tablespoons lemon juice
4 cups water
1 1/2 teaspoons vanilla

**Topping:**
1 pint whipping cream

# Ravani Cake

*In the city of Veria in northern Greece, there is a family famous for its Ravani cake. People travel for miles around to enjoy this famed dessert. The recipe is a closely held family secret—this is as close we could get!*

1/2 pound butter, melted
7 eggs, beaten
1 cup sugar
1 cup flour
2 cups farina (Cream of Wheat)
2 teaspoons baking powder
grated rind from 1 lemon or orange
1 teaspoon vanilla extract

**Syrup:**
2 cups water
2 cups sugar
juice of 1 lemon

Combine syrup ingredients and boil for 20 minutes. Cool before spooning over cake.

Meanwhile, combine the melted butter, eggs and sugar and mix well. Mix together the flour, baking powder and farina; add to egg mixture. Add flavoring and mix until well blended. Butter a 9×13-inch pan, sprinkle with a little farina and pour the batter into pan. Bake at 350 degrees for about 30 minutes. While still hot, spoon cooled syrup over cake. Let stand 6 hours or overnight before serving.

# Festival Karithopita

*Our wonderfully moist cake filled with walnuts and spices, a festival favorite!*

Boil syrup for 30 minutes and cool.

Preheat oven to 350 degrees (325 in a convection oven). Mix together walnuts, Zweibak and cinnamon. Set aside. Cream butter with mixer until light. Add yolks. Beat well. Add sugar, baking powder, baking soda and orange rind, beating well. Stir in nut mixture and set batter aside. Beat egg whites until stiff. Fold batter into whites.

Pour into greased 11×19-inch pan. (Recipe can be cut in half—use a 9×13-inch pan instead.) Bake for 1 hour. Cool 10 minutes and spoon 2 cups cooled syrup over hot cake. Serve cooled.

This cake can be frozen: Cut into diamond shapes or triangles. Place in foil cups and freeze, packaging well. Thaw and serve.

Yields 40 large pieces or 80 medium size for buffet table.

3 3/4 cups walnuts, chopped
2 1/4 cups Zweibak, finely ground
1 1/2 teaspoons cinnamon
l 1/2 pounds butter
18 eggs, separated
3 cups sugar
4 1/2 teaspoons baking powder
3/4 teaspoon baking soda
1/4 cup orange rind

**Syrup:**
3 cups sugar
5 cups water
3 tablespoons lemon juice

# Nut Cake Supreme (Karithopita)

*Ground walnuts, Zweibak crumbs, butter and eggs—and no flour—combine to make a delicious spicy cake.*

2 cups walnuts, finely ground
1/2 cup almonds, finely ground
1 box Zweibak toast, crushed
3 teaspoons baking powder
1/2 teaspoon baking soda
dash cinnamon
1 pound butter
12 eggs, separated
2 cups sugar
juice of one large orange

**Syrup:**
2 cups sugar
1 cup water
1 slice lemon

Make syrup: combine sugar, water and lemon and boil five minutes. Allow to cool.

Meanwhile, bring together the nuts and toast. Add baking powder, soda and cinnamon; set aside. In large bowl, beat butter until light. Add egg yolks and beat well. Add sugar and orange juice and continue beating until well blended. Add nut mixture and blend thoroughly. Beat egg whites until stiff and fold into nut mixture. Pour into buttered 10×15-inch pan.

Bake at 350 degrees about 45 minutes to 1 hour, until cake tests done with toothpick inserted into the center. While cake is still hot, cut into desired pieces and slowly pour cooled syrup over cake. Allow to cool thoroughly before serving.

# Quick & Easy Nut Cake (Karithopita)

*A quick, spicy Americanized version of a traditional Greek dessert.*

Combine all syrup ingredients and simmer slowly for 20 minutes. Cool.

Meanwhile, mix together all cake ingredients until well blended. Pour into greased 9×13-inch pan and bake at 350 degrees for 30 to 40 minutes, until cake tests done with a toothpick inserted into the center. Cool cake slightly and slowly pour cooled syrup over top. Allow to stand 4 to 6 hours before cutting.

2 cups Bisquick
1 cup corn oil
1 cup sugar
1 cup chopped walnuts
4 eggs, beaten
1/4 teaspoon ground cloves
1/4 teaspoon cinnamon
1/4 teaspoon nutmeg
1 teaspoon baking powder
1 teaspoon baking soda
1 cup milk
grated rind of 1/2 orange

**Syrup:**
1 1/3 cups sugar
1 1/3 cups water
1 teaspoon honey
1 slice orange

# Nut Cake (Melahrino)

*A lighter version of the spicy nut cake—made without the butter.*

2 cups crushed Zweibak crumbs
2 cups chopped walnuts or pecans
1 teaspoon cinnamon
1/2 teaspoon allspice
1/2 teaspoon salt
2 teaspoons baking powder
8 eggs, separated
1 cup sugar
2 teaspoons vanilla

**Syrup:**
4 cups water
3 cups sugar
1 thick orange slice

Combine syrup ingredients and boil for 20 minutes. Cool.

Combine first six ingredients and blend thoroughly. Set aside. In large bowl, beat egg yolks until light, add sugar and vanilla and continue to beat until a light lemon color. Add to dry ingredients, mixing well. In a separate bowl, beat egg whites until stiff. Fold into nut mixture.

Pour into a well-buttered 9×13-inch pan. Bake at 325 degrees for 30 minutes, or until cake tests done with a toothpick inserted into the center comes out clean. Pour cool syrup over cake slowly so it may be completely absorbed. Let stand 6 hours before serving. Cut into diamond shapes. Yields about 40 pieces.

Can be frozen.

# Sponge Cake

*A very light cake with the added flavor of your favorite liqueur.*

Prepare syrup: Boil all ingredients for 20 to 30 minutes. Let syrup cool completely.

Beat egg yolks until light in color. Add sugar and beat 5 minutes. Then add rest of the ingredients one at a time beating after each. Beat whites in separate bowl until stiff. Fold yolk mixture into whites and pour into a 10×15-inch baking pan. Bake at 350 degrees for 40 to 45 minutes. Pour cold syrup over hot cake. Cut into squares or diamond shapes.

10 eggs, separated
2 cups sugar
2 oranges squeezed and grated
2 cups semolina or farina
1/4 cup liqueur (Amaretto or other)

**Syrup:**
2 cups sugar
1 1/2 cups water
2 tablespoons lemon juice

# Whipped Cream Cake (Santiyi)

*A layered cake filled with apricot preserves and covered with cream.*

4 cups flour
1/2 pound sweet butter
6 eggs separated
2 cups sugar
1/2 cup cold milk
1 teaspoon baking soda
1/2 teaspoon lemon juice
16 ounces whipping cream
16-ounce jar apricot preserves
8 ounces almonds finely grated

**Syrup:**
2 cups sugar
1 1/2 cup water
2 tablespoons lemon juice

Prepare syrup first. Bring sugar, water and lemon juice to a full boil and let boil on low heat for approximately 30 to 45 minutes. Let cool completely.

Beat butter, egg yolks and sugar for 5 minutes. In separate bowl beat whites until stiff. Fold egg mixture into whites. Mix baking soda in milk and ½ teaspoon lemon juice. Add to eggs alternating with the flour and beating on low speed until well blended.

Place on two 8-inch round greased baking pans and bake at 350 degrees until brown and a toothpick placed in center comes out clean.

When cakes are done pour cool syrup on both cakes while cake is still hot. Turn one cake upside down onto a plate. Spread preserves on top of cake evenly to cover. Place the other cake on top of preserves and cover second layer with the whipped cream. Sprinkle with almonds.

# Orange Torte

*An easy cake to make—flavored with sweet orange and crunchy almonds on top.*

Beat butter and shortening, add sugar and beat until light. Add egg yolks, vanilla and rind, mixing thoroughly. Sift together flour and baking powder and add alternately with milk, blending well. Beat egg whites until stiff and fold into batter.

Pour into greased and floured 10-inch tube pan. Bake at 350 degrees for 1 hour. Cool 10 minutes, remove from pan. When completely cool, spoon hot syrup slowly over cake.

Combine syrup ingredients and boil 15 minutes. Spoon over cake. Garnish with sliced almonds.

4 eggs separated
1/2 cup butter
1/2 cup vegetable shortening
2 cups sugar
1 teaspoon vanilla
grated rind of 1 orange
3 cups flour
4 teaspoons baking powder
1 cup milk

**Syrup:**
1 cup sugar
1 cup fresh orange juice
sliced almonds

# Saint Phanourios Cake (Fanouropita)

*Saint Phanourios is the finder of lost articles. When an item is lost, this cake is baked to ask the saint's help in finding it. Traditionally, this cake is baked on Saint Phanourios Day, August 27, and the baker makes a wish for good fortune. Some young women bake this cake to ask Saint Phanourios for help finding a good husband.*

1 1/4 cups corn oil
2 1/2 cups sugar
1 1/4 cups warm water
1/2 cup orange juice
grated rind of 1 orange
1/2 teaspoon ground cloves
1/2 teaspoon ground cinnamon
3 teaspoons baking powder
4 to 5 1/2 cups flour
1/2 cup chopped walnuts
1/4 cup sesame seeds

Combine 4 cups of flour with the baking powder and spices and set aside. Beat together the oil and sugar until well mixed, add water, orange rind, orange juice and walnuts and continue to mix well. Blend in the dry ingredients until a smooth batter is formed. If it appears too thin, add more flour about 2 tablespoons at a time. Pour batter into a well buttered 10×14-inch pan, sprinkle with sesame seeds. Bake at 350 degrees 45 to 50 minutes until it tests done. Cool before cutting.

# Apricot Cake (Pasta Flora)

*Tasty and rich pastry filled with your favorite jam.*

Preheat oven to 350 degrees. Beat butter until soft and creamy. Add eggs and beat until well blended, approximately 3 minutes. Add sugar and beat for 5 minutes on medium speed. Add flour, baking powder, vanilla and cognac and beat on medium speed. Mixture will be like a thick dough but should feel soft and should not stick to hands.

Place mixture on a 13×9-inch pan. Save some of the dough to make lace strips on top. Spread dough on bottom of pan. Place apricot jam over dough to cover completely.

From remaining dough that was saved make long thin strips ¼-inch thick to fit the length of the pan, as far apart as you like, 3 or 4 strips long. Repeat the same on the width side of the pan, 5 or 6 strips long. Bake for approximately 1 hour until brown on top, or when a toothpick inserted into center of the cake comes out clean. Cut cake into square serving pieces.

1/2 pound sweet butter
3 eggs
2 cups sugar
4 cups flour
1/2 teaspoon baking powder
1 teaspoon vanilla
1/4 cup cognac
2 pounds apricot jam

# Cornmeal Cake (Bobota)

*Prepare a simple cornbread and enhance it with fruit, nuts, and spices for a very special cake.*

1/4 cup butter
1/2 cup vegetable shortening
1 cup sugar
4 eggs
rind of 2 large oranges
3 tablespoons whiskey
1/4 teaspoon baking soda
6 teaspoons baking powder
2 cups flour
1/2 teaspoon salt
1/2 cup yellow cornmeal
1/4 teaspoon cloves
1 1/2 teaspoons cinnamon
1/4 teaspoon nutmeg
1 1/2 cups orange juice
1/2 cup currants
milk

**Syrup:**
1 1/2 cups sugar
3/4 cup water
3 teaspoons honey

Cream butter and shortening with sugar until light. Add eggs, one at a time, beating well. Add grated rind. Combine whiskey and baking soda and add to batter. Sift together flour, baking powder, salt and cornmeal. Add spices and sift again. Take 1 teaspoon dry ingredients and mix with currants. Add flour mixture alternately with orange juice, blending well. Add enough milk to make a loose batter. Blend in currants. Pour into well greased 10×14-inch pan; bake at 375 degrees for 40 minutes. Cool. Top with syrup.

**Syrup:** Combine and boil over medium heat 10 minutes. Cool to lukewarm and slowly spoon over cooled cake.

# Lenten Cake (Ftohiko)

*During Lent, Orthodox Christians give up many foods, including eggs and milk. This easy dessert is a nice way to finish a Lenten meal without breaking the fast.*

Mix first five ingredients together. Then sift flour, spices, salt and baking powder together. Combine with first five ingredients, blending well then blend in all remaining ingredients in order. Divide batter into two greased 9×13-inch pans. Bake at 350 degrees for 45 minutes on top rack of oven. Remove from oven and sprinkle with powdered sugar. When cool, cut into squares or bars.

Recipe may easily be cut in half.

1 1/2 cups corn oil
1 1/2 cups hot water
1 1/2 cups orange juice
3 teaspoons baking soda
2 tablespoons whiskey
4 1/2 cups flour
1 teaspoon cinnamon
1/4 teaspoon ground cloves
1/4 teaspoon nutmeg
1/2 teaspoon allspice
pinch of salt
2 teaspoons baking powder
rind of 2 oranges
rind of 2 lemons
4 cups chopped nuts
4 cups raisins

# Festival Kourabiedes

*These are the classic Greek wedding cookies; they are also served on holidays such as Christmas and Easter. Light, buttery and deliciously sweet with a generous coating of powdered sugar. You and your guests will love them!*

1 pound unsalted butter, clarified
1/2 cup powdered sugar
1 egg yolk
1 teaspoon baking powder
2 tablespoons brandy
1 teaspoon vanilla
4 cups flour
1 cup finely chopped nuts, optional
(toasted almonds)
Additional powdered sugar for
dusting

Cream butter in electric mixer until light and fluffy. Add powdered sugar and continue beating until very light. Blend in egg yolk. Add brandy, vanilla and baking powder, mixing well. Add flour a little at a time to make a soft, pliable dough. Knead in chopped nuts if desired. Pinch off dough (about one to two tablespoons). Form into balls, then flatten to ¾-inch thickness, making rounds, crescents, or any desired shape. Place on ungreased cookie sheets, preferably on parchment paper.

Bake at 325 degrees for 35 to 40 minutes, until golden brown. (To test for doneness, cut cookie in half and see that it is baked through) Remove from oven and cool for 10 minutes. Sift powdered sugar on sheets of wax paper, or tray. Place cookies directly on powdered sugar and sprinkle generously with additional powdered sugar. When cool, place on plate to serve. These cookies hold up very well and are better after the first day.

They can be stored in a cool place, or may be frozen.

# Kourabiedes with Almonds

*These delicate cookies come in a variety of shapes, including the crescent, which was forced on the Greeks during the Turkish occupation. Today, they are traditionally shaped into balls, an 'S,' or even in cookie-cutter shapes.*

1 pound clarified butter
1/4 cup powdered sugar
1 egg yolk
2 tablespoon brandy
2 teaspoon baking powder
1/4 cup cornstarch
4 to 5 cups sifted flour
3/4 cup chopped almonds, toasted
   (if desired)
additional powdered sugar

Measure 1 full pound of clarified butter and beat at high speed with electric mixer until almost white. Add ¼ cup powdered sugar and egg yolk and beat for additional 2 minutes. Blend in the liquid ingredients. Combine half the flour with cornstarch and baking powder and gradually add to mixture. Add enough flour to make a soft dough. If adding toasted almonds, knead them into the dough thoroughly.

Pinch off small amounts of dough and shape into small balls, or you may flatten into a round and use cookie cutter to cut into shapes desired. Place on ungreased cookie sheet and bake at 325 degrees for 25 minutes. Cut a cookie to test if done. When baked, remove from pan and lay hot cookies on waxed paper sprinkled liberally with powdered sugar. Sift additional sugar over the tops. Allow to cool completely before serving. Best if made the day before since the flavor improves on standing.

# Kourabiedes with Pecans

*Take the buttery cookie and fill it with chopped nuts of your choice. Very popular for all festive occasions.*

1 pound unsalted butter or
   unsalted margarine
8 tablespoons sugar
2 teaspoons vanilla
2 teaspoons baking powder
4 cups chopped pecans
4 cups flour
powdered sugar

Melt butter and allow to cool. Add sugar and beat well. Add vanilla and pecans. Sift baking powder with 2 cups flour and add to mixture. Use enough additional flour to make a soft dough. Shape into small balls, place on ungreased cookie sheets and bake at 325 degrees for 30 to 40 minutes. While still hot, sprinkle with powdered sugar. Let cool and sprinkle with additional powdered sugar.

## CLARIFIED BUTTER

Clarified butter is used extensively in Greek cooking because it will tolerate high heat without burning. This is especially important when using delicate filo dough.

Melt butter in medium-sized saucepan on low heat until it foams, about 10 minutes. Watch carefully to avoid browning or burning. Remove from heat and let stand two minutes while milk solids settle to bottom and salt crystals settle on top.

Using a tablespoon, skim off the salt crystals and discard. Slowly pour the butterfat into a small bowl, being careful not to disturb the unwanted milk curds which have sunk to the bottom. Use a teaspoon to skim the last of the fat.

**Note:** Butter can be clarified in a microwave oven in glass or plastic bowl. Microwave on high until butter melts, about three minutes. Allow to cool in refrigerator or freezer. When solid, unmold and wash under cold running water.

# Festival Koulourakia

*These cookies come in many shapes: twist, wreath, or 'S' like a snake—made by the Minoans, who worshipped the healing powers of the serpent.*

Beat cooled clarified butter with sugar until light and fluffy. Slowly blend in eggs. Beat in vanilla and brandy. Add the baking powder to 2 cups flour and add to mixture. Continue adding enough flour to form a soft, pliable dough. Pinch off dough and roll into rope and twist. Place on ungreased cookie sheet. Beat egg yolk with a little water and brush tops of cookies, sprinkle with sesame seeds. Bake at 325 degrees for 15 to 25 minutes, until rosy. Cool on wire racks. Store in covered container.

1 pound unsalted butter, clarified
1 1/2 cups sugar
5 large eggs or 4 eggs and 2 egg yolks
3 teaspoons vanilla
2 tablespoons brandy
4 teaspoons baking powder
4 to 5 cups flour
egg yolk
sesame seeds

# Orange Koulourakia

*Zesty orange peel flavors this version.*

1 pound butter
1 1/2 cups sugar
9 eggs
1 ounce whiskey
1 teaspoon vanilla
grated rind of 1 large orange
8 cups flour
8 teaspoons baking powder

Cream butter and sugar together for 10 minutes. Add 8 eggs, one at a time, beating well. Add whiskey, vanilla and orange rind and blend thoroughly. Sift baking powder with flour. Add a little at a time to creamed mixture and blend by hand. If dough is too soft to handle, add another 2 tablespoons of flour. Pinch off pieces of dough and roll into rope and shape into ring. Place on greased cookie sheets. Beat remaining egg yolk slightly with a little water added and brush cookie tops. Bake at 350 degrees for 20 to 25 minutes.

# Sesame Koulourakia

*This version uses whipping cream instead of butter.*

Toast sesame seeds in 350-degree oven for 10 minutes, or in a heavy skillet until lightly colored. Set aside.

Sift together dry ingredients, except sugar, and set aside. Cream butter and gradually add the sugar and cream well. Add egg and vanilla and beat well. Add the dry ingredients to the butter mixture, alternating with the whipping cream, blending well after each addition with a wooden spoon until you have a soft dough that can be easily handled.

Pinch off small amount of dough and roll into cigar shape or into a rope and twist. Brush with egg and roll in sesame seed. Bake at 350 degrees for 25 to 30 minutes. Cool on wire rack.

1/2 pound sesame seeds
3 cups flour
2 teaspoons baking powder
1/4 teaspoon nutmeg
1/4 teaspoon cinnamon
1/2 teaspoon salt
1/2 cup butter
1/2 cup sugar
1 egg
1 teaspoon vanilla extract
1 1/4 cup whipping cream
beaten egg for topping

# Festival Melomacarona

*A fragrant, spicy cookie was brought by the Venetians to the Ionian islands in the 14th century. The name comes from the fact that this is the first cookie to sell out at the annual Santa Barbara Greek Festival!*

1 cup butter at room temperature
3/4 cup sugar
2 cups corn oil
1 cup orange juice
1 teaspoon baking soda
1/4 cup orange zest
2 teaspoons cinnamon
8 cups flour (approximately)
Finely chopped walnuts and
    cinnamon for topping

**Syrup:**
2 cups water
4 cups sugar
1 cup honey
2 teaspoon lemon juice

Cream butter, oil and sugar together in mixer at high speed until light. Beat in the cinnamon and zest. Combine the baking soda with orange juice and add quickly to the mixture. Blend well. Begin adding the flour until the dough is soft, pliable and can be easily handled. Pinch off 2 tablespoons of dough and shape into oblong rolls, flatten top and taper ends. Place on ungreased baking sheets Bake at 325 degrees for 35 to 45 minutes, then test for doneness. (to test, cut cookie in half to see if it is baked through) Continue baking until center is cooked.

Remove from oven and cool.

Boil all syrup ingredients together for 10 minutes. Remove from heat. Dip cooled cookies in hot syrup being careful not to crowd pan, first on one side, then turn over. Remove with slotted spoon and place on trays. Sprinkle with a mixture of ground walnuts and cinnamon. Cool.

Makes 80 cookies. These keep in the freezer very well.

# Melomacarona with Filling

*Another variation of the spicy cookie—this one with a nut filling.*

Beat shortening, oil, sugar, salt and vanilla for at least ½ hour. Add orange juice. Sift flour, soda and baking powder and add flour mixture gradually to creamed mixture, mixing by hand until dough can easily be shaped. (May require more flour)

Combine all filling ingredients and blend thoroughly. This will be a thick mixture.

Take small amount of dough (size of large walnut), flatten and add ¼ teaspoon filling, fold and mold into crescents. Bake on ungreased pan at 450 degrees for 10 minutes. Cool.

Bring syrup ingredients—sugar, water, lemon rind, cloves and cinnamon stick—to boil until slightly thickened. Remove from heat, add honey, lemon juice and whiskey. Dip cookies in very hot syrup until syrup penetrates. Drain and sprinkle while hot with additional ground cinnamon and chopped walnuts.

**Note:** Can be frozen without syrup and can also be kept in refrigerator for weeks. Refrigerate any remaining syrup. Makes about 80 cookies.

1 cup shortening
5 cups flour
1 cup corn oil
1 teaspoon baking soda
1 cup sugar
1 teaspoon baking powder
1/2 teaspoon salt
1 teaspoon vanilla
1 cup orange juice

**Filling:**
1/2 pound walnuts, chopped
    coarsely
3 tablespoon honey
1/4 teaspoon ground cloves

**Syrup:**
2 cups sugar
2 cinnamon sticks
1 1/2 cups water
1 cup honey
Rind of 1/2 lemon
2 tablespoons lemon juice
5 whole cloves
2 tablespoons whiskey (if desired)

# Melomacarona with Sesame Seed

*This spicy cookie has sesame seeds added for taste and texture.*

2 cups corn oil
1 stick butter
2 tablespoons vegetable shortening
1 cup orange juice
1 cup sugar
2 eggs
3 tablespoons honey
1 cup crushed nutmeats
1 cup sesame seed meal*
6 cups flour
2 tablespoons cinnamon
1 teaspoon nutmeg
1 teaspoon ground cloves
3 rounded teaspoons baking
    powder

**Syrup:**
2 cups sugar
1/2 cup honey
juice of 1/2 lemon
2 cups boiling water

**Topping:**
sesame seeds
chopped nuts
cinnamon
sugar

*Sesame meal is obtained by
 pulsing sesame seed in processor
 or blender until mealy.

Beat together first five ingredients, then add eggs, honey, nutmeats and sesame seed meal. Sift together flour, cinnamon, nutmeg, cloves, and baking powder and add to mixture.

Knead slightly and add more flour if necessary (up to 2 cups) to allow shaping of cookie. Pinch off about 2 tablespoons of dough and shape into oblong rolls. Place on ungreased cookie sheet and bake at 350 degrees for 30 to 35 minutes.

Remove from oven, dip cookies in warm honey syrup, being careful not to allow to soak. In large plate, have a mixture of crushed sesame seeds, chopped nuts, cinnamon and sugar. Roll warm cookies in mixture and place on rack to cool.

**Syrup:** Combine ingredients and boil at least 5 minutes. Keep warm.

# Spice Bars (Finikia)

*Similar to the Melomacarona, but uses corn oil instead of some—or all—of the butter.*

Blend oil, sugar and seasonings. Add orange juice, then 2 cups flour blended with baking powder and soda. Continue to add flour until a smooth dough is formed, not too stiff. Gently knead in the chopped nuts.

Pinch off small portions of dough and form into little oblong rolls. Place on ungreased cookie sheet and bake at 375 degrees for 35 minutes, until slight browned. While still warm, dip into syrup.

**Syrup:** Combine ingredients and boil at least 5 minutes. Dip finikia into syrup being careful not to allow to become soggy. Place on rack to cool. Makes 4 dozen cookies.

If desired, the finikia may be rolled in a mixture of sugar and cinnamon after dipping into syrup. Let cool.

1/2 cup sugar
1/2 cup orange juice
1 teaspoon grated orange rind
2 cups corn oil (or 1 cup butter and
   1 cup oil)
2 teaspoons cinnamon
1/4 teaspoon nutmeg
1 teaspoon baking powder
1/2 teaspoon baking soda
2 cups chopped walnuts or pecans
about 7 cups flour

**Syrup:**
2 cups sugar
1/2 cup honey
juice of 1/2 lemon
2 cups boiling water

# Paximadia I—Toasted Cookie Slices

*This cookie was originally brought to bereaved families, but has become very popular today for breakfast or afternoon tea. It is similar to the familiar Italian biscotti. A wonderful, tasty dunking cookie.*

1/2 pound unsalted butter
1/2 cup corn oil
1 1/4 cup sugar
1/2 teaspoon baking soda
2 teaspoon vanilla
3 teaspoon brandy
3 eggs
1/2 cup almonds or pecans, ground
6 cups flour (approximately)

Cream butter, oil and sugar until light and fluffy. Add eggs one at a time, then almonds, vanilla and baking soda and beat until well blended. Add enough of the flour to make a soft, pliable dough.

Divide into thirds and shape and pat into 3 long, narrow strips, about 2 inches wide, to fit a 12×17-inch baking sheet. Bake at 350 degrees for 30 minutes.

Keep oven hot and remove loaves to board. Cut into ¾-inch slices. Place in pan, cut side down, and return to oven and bake 15 minutes more, till lightly toasted. Cool on racks and store in airtight container. Can be frozen.

# Paximadia II—Orange Spice Cookies

*A Greek version of biscotti; serve these cookies with coffee for a mid-afternoon treat.*

Beat together the oil, eggs, and sugar until well mixed. Add nuts, orange rind, milk, and dry ingredients and blend well. Pour batter to a depth of 1 inch, measuring depth with a toothpick. Bake at 350 degrees 20 to 25 minutes, until tests done. Let stand 5 minutes. Remove from pans and cool completely on wire racks. Slice ⅜-inch thick and lay on cookie sheets.

Preheat oven to 350 degrees and toast slices 10 minutes on each side until dry. Makes about 6 dozen.

1 1/2 cups corn oil
6 eggs
1 1/2 cups sugar
1 cup walnuts, coarsely chopped
grated rind of 1 orange
1/2 cup milk
2 1/2 cups flour
2 teaspoons baking powder

# Paximadia III—Toasted Spice Cookie Slices

*The combination of cinnamon and cloves gives a spicy bite to these crunchy cookies.*

4 cups flour
1 1/2 teaspoons cinnamon
1/2 teaspoon ground cloves
4 teaspoons baking powder
1/2 cup corn oil
1 stick butter (1/2 cup) softened
1 cup sugar
3 eggs
1/2 cup chopped walnuts or
 pecans

Combine the flour, spices, and baking powder and set aside.

Combine the oil and butter in a large bowl and beat until blended. Slowly add sugar and continue beating until light. Add eggs one at a time and continue beating until creamy. On low speed, slowly add the dry ingredients, then the nutmeats.

Shape into small loaves (about four) and bake at 325 degrees for 30 minutes. Remove from oven and place each loaf on breadboard.

Increase oven temperature to 350 degrees and cut each loaf into ½-inch slices and place in rows, cut-side down on baking sheets. Return to oven and toast for about 15 minutes until browned. Cool on wire racks and store in covered container. Makes about 5 to 6 dozen.

# Custard Tart (Custard Bougatsa)

*A wonderful way to start your morning is with a serving of Bougatsa with your coffee or tea. Try both the custard, customary to northern Greece, or the cheese bougatsa from Crete.*

Bring to boil milk and sugar. Add butter and Cream of Wheat. Reduce heat and cook, stirring continuously, until thickened, about 10 minutes. Remove from heat and cool slightly. Beat eggs with vanilla and mix in quickly. Set aside.

Layer half the filo in a 9×13-inch pan, buttering each layer and having filo extend over edge of pan. Pour in the filling and fold over extended filo to enclose the filling. Cover with remaining filo, buttering each layer. Score the top sheets with a sharp knife into 3-inch squares, and bake in preheated 350 degree oven for 25 to 30 minutes, until filo is golden and filling is set.

Remove from oven, allow to cool slightly. Cut along scored lines into serving pieces and dust with powdered sugar and serve warm. Makes a tasty breakfast treat.

**Custard:**
1 quart milk
1/2 cup sugar
1 tablespoon butter
1/3 cup quick Cream of Wheat
4 large eggs, beaten
1 1/2 teaspoons vanilla

1/2 pound filo
1 stick unsalted butter, melted
powdered sugar

# Cheese Bougatsa

*A more savory filling—and just as delicious.*

8 ounces cream cheese
1 pound ricotta cheese
1 cup small curd cottage cheese
2 tablespoons sugar
1 egg
dash nutmeg
1 pound filo dough
2 sticks melted unsalted butter

Combine the cheeses, sugar, egg and nutmeg and beat at high speed with electric mixer for about 1 minute. Set aside and prepare filo.

Stack 4 sheets buttered filo on board to form a base. Lay 2 sheets at right angles over the center to make a diamond base, not a square and brush the center of the sheets with butter. Spread about ⅓ of the filling in the center base to form a square. Fold the top filo over the cheese and brush with butter. Continue folding the filo and brushing with butter. Lift the square and invert onto a cookie sheet, brush top with butter and set aside.

Continue the same manner with remaining filo and filling until you have 3 pites. Bake at 350 degrees for 20 to 25 minutes, until filo is puffed and golden. Cut into squares and sprinkle with powdered sugar. Serve warm.

# Sweet Karpathian Tarts

*From the Dodecanese Islands in southern Greece come these delicious cheese tarts.*

Beat together butter, shortening, and sugar. Add eggs, orange juice and orange rind. Blend in cake flour sifted and baking powder

This makes a rich cookie dough. If it seems a little stiff, knead it with some cooking oil on your hands.

Mix all filling ingredients together thoroughly.

Roll out small portion of dough to make about a 3 ½-inch square. Put some filling in the center. Fold over edges to enclose filling, leaving some filling showing through center. Press filling on corners to seal. Brush with beaten egg mixed with a little water. Place on greased cookie sheets. Bake about 15 minutes at 350 degrees until lightly browned.

Yields about 85 pieces. Freezes well.

1 pound butter
4 tablespoons shortening
2 1/2 cups sugar
6 eggs
1 cup orange juice
1 tablespoon grated orange rind
10 cups cake flour
10 teaspoons baking powder

**Filling:**
5 eggs, well beaten
1 pound cream cheese
3 pounds ricotta cheese
1 cup sugar
1/2 teaspoon nutmeg
1 teaspoon cinnamon

# Loukoumathes

*This delightful treat was at one time the prize presented to winners at sporting events.*

1 package dry yeast
1/4 cup warm water
1 cup warm milk
1/4 cup sugar
2 eggs, beaten
1/2 cup melted butter
1/2 teaspoon salt
3 cups flour
cooking oil
1 cup honey
2 tablespoons water
1/3 cup chopped walnuts
cinnamon

Add yeast to warm water. In a large bowl, pour warm milk, add sugar and salt. Stir in yeast, beaten eggs, melted butter and beat well. Gradually add enough flour, beating continuously, until batter is soft and spongy. Batter will be sticky. Cover and let rise until double in size.

Heat 2 to 3 inches oil in heavy pan to 375 degrees. Fill palm of left hand with dough and squeeze, allowing mixture to come through thumb and first finger, into a small round ball (loukoumatha). Dip tablespoon into cold oil and with right hand, scoop mixture from the left hand, dropping it gently into the hot oil. Fry only a few at a time and turn as soon as loukoumathes are browned, about 7 minutes. Remove from oil and drain on paper towels.

Heat honey and water in saucepan. Dip loukoumathes in honey, turning quickly to cover, and place on platter. Sprinkle with nuts and cinnamon.

**Note:** These can be reheated in a warm oven before drizzling with honey.

# Easy Loukoumathes

*The streamlined version of the timeless recipe for modern cooks with good taste and too little time.*

Soften yeast in ½ cup warm water. In large bowl combine the dry ingredients. Add the remaining water, yeast mixture and egg and beat with spoon until blended. Let rise 3 to 4 hours. Batter should be fairly soft and spongy. You may need to add additional water, up to ⅓ cup.

2 cups flour
2 cups Bisquick
2 cups water, or more
1 package yeast
1/4 teaspoon salt
1 beaten egg

Heat 2 to 3 inches oil in heavy pan to 375 degrees. Fill palm of left hand with dough and squeeze, allowing mixture to come through thumb and first finger, into a small round ball. Dip tablespoon into cold oil and with right hand, scoop mixture from the left hand, dropping it gently into the hot oil. Fry only a few at a time and turn as soon as loukoumathes are browned, about 6 or 7 minutes. Remove from oil and drain on paper towels. Drizzle with honey and serve warm.

You can also shape loukoumathes with two spoons. Dip spoon in cold oil and spoon batter into hot oil, releasing batter with the other spoon.

# Crispy Honey Curls (Diples)

*In the days of the grandmothers, the Diples were rolled thin with a long stick like a broom handle called a plasti. This was an all-day project. Today's cooks have access to the pasta machine, making the whole process so much simpler. Of course, frying the diples is still a challenge. These light, crispy, sweet treats are called by various names, the most familiar being Diples, but in Crete they are called Xerotigana. No matter what their name, they are delicious!*

6 eggs
1/2 teaspoon salt
4 cups flour
cinnamon
ground walnuts
vegetable oil for frying

**Syrup:**
4 cups honey
1 cup water

Beat eggs slightly, add salt and beat again. Using your hands, add flour, knead in enough flour to make a smooth consistency that does not stick to your hands. Continue kneading until dough is very smooth.

Take half the dough (keeping the remaining dough covered to keep from drying out) and roll out on floured board. Cut into strips about 2×4 inches. Using a pasta machine, roll through widest setting, then through middle setting, and finally through narrowest opening. Cut into 8-inch strips, and keep covered.

In electric skillet, have enough oil to cover about 2½-inch depth. Heat to 375 degrees. Stretch strip of dough slightly and drop into hot oil. Using two forks, turn dough over and roll quickly in jelly-roll fashion into the oil before it becomes crisp. Fry until lightly brown. Drain in colander, then on absorbent towels.

**Syrup:** Boil honey and water for 5 minutes.

When diples are cool, dip in warm honey syrup and drain in colander. Place on platter and sprinkle with cinnamon and ground walnuts. Makes about 75 diples.

**Note:** Dough may be cut into 2-inch strips and shaped into bows or knots and fried until crispy.

Diples can be stored in covered container for several weeks then dipped in warm syrup to serve.

# Rice Pudding (Rizogalo)

*The original "comfort" food, rice pudding for dessert or a snack. It's often found on the menu in Greek restaurants.*

Combine all ingredients except cinnamon, in a large pot and bring to boil, stirring constantly. Reduce heat and cook until slightly thickened and rice is tender (at least 45 minutes) stirring continuously. Pour into serving bowls and sprinkle with cinnamon. Makes 12 servings, ½ cup each.

2 quarts milk
1 cup raw rice (not converted)
1 cup sugar
2 eggs, beaten
1 tablespoon butter
1 teaspoon vanilla
cinnamon

# Creamy Rice Pudding

*Another mother's version of the classic treat.*

Spray pot with non-sticking spray. Combine rice and liquids, bring to simmer and cook until rice is tender, about 45 minutes, stirring frequently. Add sugar, mixing thoroughly. Add some rice mixture to egg yolks slowly, beating constantly, then return to remaining rice in sauce pot. Simmer 5 minutes until thick. Pour into large bowl or individual bowls. Sprinkle with cinnamon. Cool and refrigerate.

3/4 cup pearl rice
5 cups milk
1 cup water
3 egg yolks, beaten
1 cup sugar
cinnamon

# Almond Dessert (Halva)

*Unlike the commercial halva made with ground sesame seeds, this family dessert features almonds and faina.*

2 cups semolina or farina
1/2 cup sugar
1 cup butter
1 cup almonds, finely chopped
4 eggs
1 teaspoon cinnamon

**Syrup:**
1/2 cup sugar
1/2 cup water
2 tablespoons lemon juice

Prepare syrup: Boil sugar, water and lemon juice for 30 minutes and let cool completely.

Beat butter and sugar for 5 minutes. Add eggs one at a time and beat after each addition. Add semolina, cinnamon and nuts. Pour into an 8×8-inch baking pan. Bake at 350 degree for 40 to 45 minutes. Pour the cold syrup over the hot halva.

Cut into squares or diamonds and serve cold.

# Spooned Halva

*This version of halva is cooled in a skillet on top of the stove.*

1/2 cup almonds, chopped
1/2 cup vegetable oil
2 cups semolina or farina
1/2 teaspoon ground cloves
1 teaspoon ground cinnamon

**Syrup:**
2 cups sugar
2 cups water
2 cinnamon sticks
2 whole cloves
2 tablespoons lemon juice

Mix almonds, oil and semolina or farina in a skillet and cook on medium heat until brown, stirring constantly. Add ground cloves and cinnamon. Mix well and set aside.

Prepare syrup: Boil sugar, water, cinnamon, cloves and lemon juice for approximately 30 minutes. Pour hot syrup into the almond mixture and mix well. Pour mixture into a gelatin mold. Refrigerate until set, about 4 to 5 hours or over night.

Serve cold.

# Kaimaki

*Although this culinary treat is not really Greek, Kaimaki, or "bubbles of cream," was developed to honor the Empress Eugénie. It became one of the outstanding desserts of Constantinople, served with a very sweet honeyed pastry such as baklava or kataifi.*

Bring one quart whipping cream to a boil over low heat in an enameled pan. With a ladle, lift out cream and pour back into the pan from shoulder height, while keeping the cream on very low heat. Keep this up for about one hour—the amount of elbow grease you have determines how high the bubbles rise. Turn off the heat and let cream remain in a warm place for about two hours or until firm. Refrigerate for at least 8 hours. With a sharp knife, cut loose bubbles of cream that have set. Cut into strips and serve atop pastry.

1 quart whipping cream

**Short-Cut Method:** In a heavy pan, gradually bring cream to a boil over very low heat. Stirring occasionally, simmer for an hour or until reduced by half. Stir in 1 to 2 tablespoons of brandy, if desired. Spread into a shallow 9-inch pan, refrigerate and serve as noted above.

# Spoon Sweets

*It is the custom in a Greek household to welcome guests with something sweet, a custom which began centuries ago with the Persians when they wanted to demonstrate hospitality. One of the first prerequisites of a Greek hostess is to prepare the tray which is presented to a guest. On the tray is a glass of cold water, a spoonful of preserves in a small glass dish and a serving of a liqueur (Masticha preferably) or a demitasse of Greek coffee.*

## ORANGE RIND PRESERVES

*Citrus fruits, when prepared properly—as this recipe reveals—have delicious flavor without any bitterness.*

4 cups navel orange rind
4 cups sugar
2 cups water

You will need thick-skinned navel oranges for this recipe. From stem to navel, cut orange peel in ½-inch strips. Place rinds in a large pot, cover with cold water and bring to a boil. Pour off the water and repeat process twice more, then drain. Take each strip of rind and roll tightly into a small roll, jelly roll style. With a clean sewing needle and heavy white thread, sew through the roll. Be sure thread is knotted on the end. Continue with rolls, threading like a necklace.

Place the sugar and water in a large saucepan and bring to a boil, stirring constantly. Cook 15 minutes then add the rinds on their strings and continue cooking. Remove the rinds when a needle will pierce them easily, but continue cooking the syrup until it reaches 220 degrees on a candy thermometer. Remove from heat, add the orange rinds on strings and the juice of 1 lemon. Cool rinds in the syrup. Cut and remove the strings and store in sealed containers.

**Note:** Grapefruit rind preserves may be prepared the same way.

## QUINCE PRESERVES

*A little tart, a little sweet—the distinctively delicate taste of the quince.*

Peel and cut quince into small pieces into a bowl of cold water with a little lemon juice squeezed in. When all fruit is cut, drain and place in large deep pot, cover with sugar and water. Bring to a boil stirring constantly until the sugar is dissolved. Reduce heat to medium and cook until the fruit is tender and the syrup thickens and reaches 220 degrees on candy thermometer, about 1 hour. Stir in the juice of 1 lemon, the almonds and rose geranium. Cool, then remove the geranium leaves and seal in airtight glass container.

4 cups quince
4 cups sugar
1 1/2 cups water
juice of 1 lemon
rose geranium leaves, if available
1/2 cup blanched, slivered almonds

## ROSE PETAL PRESERVES

*A monastery in the Peloponnese is famous for its rose petal preserves. Now you can make your own at home!*

Snip off white base of rose petals, using only the top parts. Put in a bowl, cover with sugar and let stand 4 hours or overnight, tossing with fork occasionally to mix sugar and petals.

Bring water to a boil in a large pot. Add sugared petals and remaining ingredients and stir gently until sugar melts. Reduce heat and simmer on medium heat for 45 minutes or until reaches 220 degrees on candy thermometer. Cover pot the last 10 minutes of cooking time. Pour into clean small jars and seal with paraffin (as for jam).

4 cups rose petals (wild, garden or florist variety)
4 cups sugar
2 cups water
1/2 cup corn syrup
3 tablespoons lemon juice
1/4 teaspoon cream of tartar

# Sesame Candy (Pasteli)

D
E
S
S
E
R
T
S

*Sesame seeds—high in Vitamin E and calcium—combine with honey for a wholesome and delicious treat.*

3 pounds high quality honey
2 pounds sesame seeds

Oil a 7×11-inch pan and place in freezer until very cold. Bring honey to boil over low heat, until thickened; stir with wooden spoon until honey is of thready consistency. Add sesame seeds and stir until bubbles form. (Be careful since mixture will spatter) Remove pan from freezer and pour mixture into pan and allow to cool completely. Invert onto board and cut into 1×2-inch pieces.

# Greek-Style Coffee

*In Greece, coffee is usually served with a glass of water. Many Greek-Americans continue the practice in the U.S. Often, when tourists simply order coffee, the waiter will serve Nescafé—or instant coffee. If you want full-strength, espresso-like Greek coffee, you must specify it, along with a desired sweetness level:* glyko *(sweet),* metrio *(medium), and* pykro *(bitter).*

Put water in a Greek coffeepot. Place over high flame. When water boils add sugar and stir well. Continue boiling and add coffee, stir well and remove immediately so as to form a heavy coat on top and to retain flavor. Put one teaspoon of the foam into each demitasse cup and pour remaining coffee filling each cup. Do not add milk or stir. Serves four.

4 demitasse cups water
4 heaping teaspoons Greek coffee
4 teaspoons sugar

To properly prepare Greek coffee, it should be cooked in a special bronze coffeepot called a *briki.* This type of pot is a must in every Greek kitchen. It is served to guests in the afternoon as a pick-me-up and at the conclusion of a meal. To be fully appreciated, Greek coffee is sipped slowly. Thick grounds will remain in the bottom of the cup. When the coffee drinker has finished, the cup is turned upside-down in the saucer and allowed to remain for several minutes. The grounds will make a pattern on the sides of the cup and can be clearly read. If the grounds are separated by wide spaces, it means a long voyage; smaller spaces, a short trip. A large blob means money, small ones mean trouble. For further details, consult a Greek grandmother.

# INDEX OF RECIPES
*In the order of their appearance*

**THE SIDEBARS**

# THE GREEK FEAST
## *Santa Barbara Style*

To order additional copies ($14.95 plus $3 shipping) of
*The Greek Feast Santa Barbara Style,* contact the publisher at:

Olympus Press
POST OFFICE BOX 2397
SANTA BARBARA, CALIFORNIA 93120
(805) 965-7200

Make checks payable to:
*The Saint Barbara Philoptochos Society*

THE SAINT BARBARA PHILOPTOCHOS SOCIETY is an important auxiliary
parish organization supporting local charities, as well as national and
international missions and ministries of the Greek Orthodox Church.

*Philoptochos* means "friends of the poor"; monies from the sale of this
cookbook will be used to further the charitable work of this ministry.

For more information about Philoptochos ministries and activities,
contact Saint Barbara Greek Orthodox Church, 1205 San Antonio Creek
Road, Santa Barbara, California 93111; (805) 683-4492.